M48 Patton

America's First "Main Battle Tank"

DAVID DOYLE

SCHIFFER MILITARY

4880 Lower Valley Road   Atglen, PA 19310

Designed by Christopher Bower
Cover design by Justin Watkinson
Type set in Impact/Minion Pro/Univers LT Std

ISBN: 978-0-7643-6783-0
Printed in India

Published by Schiffer Publishing, Ltd.
4880 Lower Valley Road
Atglen, PA 19310
Phone: (610) 593-1777; Fax: (610) 593-2002
Email: Info@schifferbooks.com
Web: www.schifferbooks.com

For our complete selection of fine books on this and related subjects, please visit our website at www.schifferbooks.com. You may also write for a free catalog.

Schiffer Publishing's titles are available at special discounts for bulk purchases for sales promotions or premiums. Special editions, including personalized covers, corporate imprints, and excerpts, can be created in large quantities for special needs. For more information, contact the publisher.

We are always looking for people to write books on new and related subjects. If you have an idea for a book, please contact us at proposals@schifferbooks.com.

Acknowledgments

This book would not have been possible without the generous help of my friends Tom Kailbourn, Scott Taylor, John Charvat, Chun Hsu, and Steve Zaloga; the staffs of the former Patton Museum, the TACOM LCMC History Office, the USMC, and the Ordnance Museum; the Grand Blanc Heritage Museum; Kevin Emdee and the late Don Moriarty. Special thanks go to my darling wife, Denise, who stood firmly by me as I labored on long into the nights to complete this work.

All vintage photos not otherwise credited are from the collections of the US National Archives and Records Administration; all photos of preserved vehicles not otherwise credited are by the author.

FSC
www.fsc.org
MIX
Paper from responsible sources
FSC® C016779

Contents

Introduction

American Locomotive Company (ALCO) began series production of the M47 90 mm gun tank, the interim tank between the M46 Pershing and the M48 Patton, in 1951. The Detroit Arsenal also manufactured M47s. The M47 had a hull and suspension similar to those of the M46, but the turret was new, and three track-support rollers were used per side, instead of the five rollers on the M46. These three ALCO M47s were photographed in September 1952. Muzzle brakes were not installed on the guns.

The M48 series of medium tank came into being driven by the need to replace the M26 Pershing, which began production late in World War II. This need for an improved medium tank, which had been studied since the waning days of World War II, reached a new level of urgency when war broke out on the Korea Peninsula in 1950. The Pershing was always considered to be underpowered. To address this, as an interim solution the M46 was introduced, which was an M26 with a new, air-cooled, twelve-cylinder Continental engine replacing the Ford GAF V-8, which itself was a variation of the GAA, which powered the much-smaller Sherman tank.

The M46 was followed by the stopgap M47, created by marrying the air-cooled Continental engine, as well as the newly designed T42 turret, to the proven M46 hull and suspension design. The pilot M47 in fact was produced using an M46 hull, although the production vehicles had hulls with increased angle of slope on the front armor.

The M46 and M47 were considered interim vehicles, and development of an all-new tank began at Chrysler in November 1950, following a meeting the previous March at which the Ordnance Committee indicated that they intended to issue a letter contract to the firm to develop a new medium tank and construct prototypes of the same.

Chrysler engineers prepared layout drawings and constructed a half-scale clay model of the proposed hull and turret, which Ordnance approved on February 2, 1951.

Finally, on February 27, Ordnance formally approved the project and issued the required characteristics for the tank, which included a four-man crew, a track width of 28 inches, and a maximum weight of 90,000 pounds. Armament was to be a new lightweight 90 mm gun. During this development stage, the tank was given the designation T48.

ALCO executives and workers pose alongside the last tank, an M47, completed at their plant. Once production of the M47s ceased at ALCO, the company closed its tank division. ALCO built 3,095 of the vehicles, while Detroit Arsenal completed 5,481 of them.

CHAPTER 1
T48/M48

On January 29, 1952, the chassis of the first of six pilot vehicles contracted for had been completed and was shipped from Chrysler's Development Department in Highland Park, Michigan, to the firm's new proving ground in Chelsea, Michigan, where it underwent testing for two weeks. At the conclusion of those tests, it was returned to Highland Park, where it was mated with the turret, which had just completed testing at that facility. It returned to Chelsea on February 27 for additional testing and observation by Army representatives.

As the engineers in Highland Park had been developing the tank, other engineers had been designing and constructing a new Chrysler tank plant in Newark, Delaware. It was in this new facility that the second pilot was constructed. That T48 was completed during December 1951 but had not been released, pending the results of testing of the Michigan tank. The second pilot was modified to incorporate improvements called for as a result of the Michigan tests, and in April 1952 it was shipped to Aberdeen Proving Ground for testing, where it arrived on April 11.

Tanks 3 and 4 were shipped to the Armor Board at Fort Knox, arriving in May and July, respectively. Tank 5 also went to Aberdeen, arriving in November, and the final pilot was assigned to the US Marine Corps.

While the T48 used the Continental AV-1790 engine and General Motors' CD-850-4 transmission, proven in the M46/47, the turret ring was enlarged as a provision for later possible upgunning. Whereas most earlier US tanks had slab-sided turrets, the turret of the T48 was rounded, affording greater ballistic protection.

The conflict in Korea made it imperative that replacement tanks be produced. Hence, the T48 was approved for production even before it was standardized. With world tension high, Chrysler was given an order for 548 tanks, and both Ford Motor Company and the Fisher Body Division of General Motors received orders for 400 each, before testing was even completed. Chrysler's Newark plant began delivering production tanks in April 1952, even as it was still delivering the pilot tanks. The tanks, originally specified at 45 tons, ultimately weighed in at between 49 and 50 tons when combat-loaded, but the world situation at the time was such that production proceeded—there was simply no time to attempt a redesign to address the weight issue. However, testing did indicate some issues that had to be resolved prior to issuing the tanks to combat units. Among these, as originally designed the engine exhaust would heat the main gun travel lock to the point that it could not be released or, at the least, required the crew to don asbestos gloves to attempt to release the lock. Testing at Fort Knox resulted in a request that a track tension idler be added between the drive sprocket and rear road wheel to minimize track throwing. The .50-caliber coaxial machine gun, originally mounted at the left of the main gun, was replaced by a .30-caliber weapon, and a direct-sight telescope replaced the .30-caliber weapon previously found to the right of the main gun.

The most serious problem found was that 120 tanks had been produced with hulls that were ballistically defective.

Nearly 1,000 T48s were produced before the production model was standardized as the "90 mm gun tank M48" on April 2, 1953. At the same time, it was officially named the Patton 48, honoring World War II general George S. Patton Jr. Fittingly, the tank was introduced into service in 1953 by the 2nd Armored Division, Patton's famed "Hell on Wheels" of World War II.

During production of these tanks, several improvements were introduced, some modest and unseen. One of the more important, and more visible, improvements was the introduction of a larger driver's hatch.

A Chrysler test driver is at the controls of a newly completed M48 90 mm gun tank at the Newark plant, in a photo released to the public on July 1, 1952. Jutting from the sides of the turret are the dome-shaped hoods for the rangefinder objectives. A Browning M2 HB .50-caliber machine gun is mounted on a support attached to the low-profile cupola.

Chrysler built its Newark Assembly Plant in Newark, Delaware, for the purpose of constructing T48 tanks. The first of that model of 90 mm gun tanks to roll off that assembly line was pilot T48 number 2, in December 1951. Here, workers are milling the cupola ring of a T48 turret marked "#36" on its side. In the background is an assembled T48, with the distinctive muzzle blast deflector used on the 90 mm guns on production T48s. This device replaced the muzzle brake employed on the pilot T48s.

Early on, the T48 tanks had a small hatch for the driver. This feature is visible on the lead tank on the Newark Assembly Plant production line. Later, the rear corners of the hatch would be extended outward, resulting in a large hatch. The swiveling door of this hatch has not yet been installed. The T48s featured a Chrysler-designed, low-silhouette commander's cupola with externally mounted .50-caliber machine gun. The track-tension idler that later would be incorporated into production M48s, below and to the front of each sprocket, are not present. Rolled track assemblies and parts bins are stacked to the sides of the assembly line.

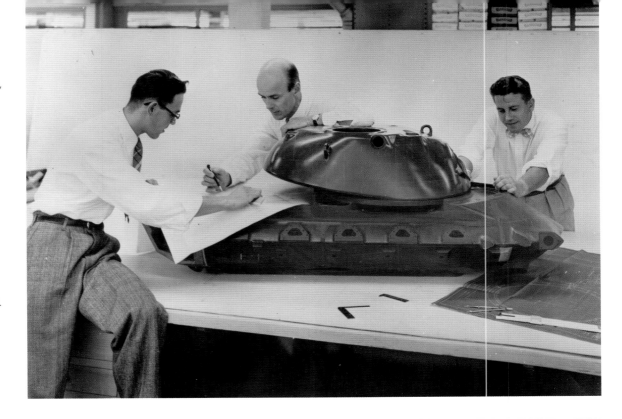

Leroy W. Pohlman, John Pietsch, and Alfred W. Bors, General Motors engineers at the Fisher Body Division plant in Grand Blanc, Michigan, are recording measurements on a scale model of hull and turret of the T48 90 mm gun tank, during preproduction planning for the vehicle. The almost dome-shaped turret was a significant departure from the turret of the M47, which had a flat top, flatter sides, and a pronounced bustle. Production of the T48s initially proceeded at the Chrysler tank plant at Newark, Delaware, which also served as the vehicle's design agency, but Ford Motor Company and Fisher Body Division subsequently manufactured the vehicles as well.

In addition to Chrysler's Newark Assembly Plant, Ford Motor Company and Fisher Body Division of General Motors' Grand Blanc, Michigan, plant produced the T48 90 mm gun tanks. An Army officer and a civilian pose next to the first T48 tank hull assembly to roll out of Fisher's Grand Blanc plant, on February 16, 1952. A curiosity of this chassis is the single track-tension idler wheel, between the rear bogie wheel and the sprocket. The T48s had five track-support rollers on each side, while production M48s would have three per side. *Grand Blanc Heritage Museum*

Inside the Grand Blanc plant, to the left are completed M48s on railroad flatcars. The turrets are traversed to the rear, and weatherproof covers have been fitted over the rear decks. In the center and right background are more M48s, being readied for shipment. Numbers are marked on the cupola (532), the turret (2998), and the bow of the hull (2981). *Grand Blanc Heritage Museum*

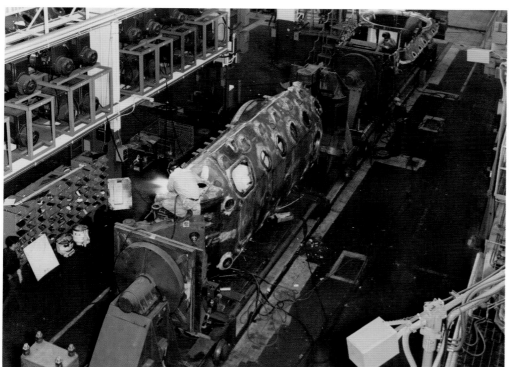

Two M48 hulls are under construction at Grand Blanc. Both units are secured to rotary jigs, which allowed the assemblies to be turned as needed. These hulls consisted of sections that were welded together. Later, a cast hull was developed. *Grand Blanc Heritage Museum*

On November 23, 1954, the Grand Blanc plant hosted the "Golden Carnival Open House" to demonstrate to the public the operations and products of the tank factory. Guests are visiting a display of Aircraft Armaments Model 30 commander's cupolas. On the large table at the center are cupola rings, a hatch door, and several cupola castings. The man to right has his hand on a cupola casting, mounted upside down on a jig. *Grand Blanc Heritage Museum*

During the Golden Carnival Open House, two cupola assemblies are mounted on test stands; the sign identifies the scene as "commander's cupola target area for .50-caliber machine gun." Panels with sighting marks on them are to the fronts of the turrets. *Grand Blanc Heritage Museum*

Turret assemblies for M48A1 tanks are mounted on so-called buildup stands during the Golden Carnival Open House. White-colored turret baskets are below the turret castings, and Model 30 commander's cupolas are mounted on the turret roofs. *Grand Blanc Heritage Museum*

Suspension parts, before and after machining, are displayed during the Golden Carnival Open House at the Grand Blanc plant. Stored in the left background are suspension arms for the bogie assemblies. *Grand Blanc Heritage Museum*

A ramp was installed to the rear of an M48 or M48A1 hull at the Golden Carnival Open House, on February 16, 1952. In the foreground on the hull top are the dual exhaust pipes of the crew heater. Part of the power plant of the tank is on display to the far right. *Grand Blanc Heritage Museum*

An M48 90 mm gun tank, with a Chrysler low-profile cupola on the turret, is on display at an event at an unidentified location, possibly in Flint, Michigan, near the Grand Blanc factory. The bore evacuator and the muzzle of the 90 mm gun have been wrapped with tape. *Grand Blanc Heritage Museum*

Ford Motor Company was another manufacturer of the T48 90 mm gun tank. An executive is standing in the commander's low-profile cupola of this example, with Ford's Highland Park power plant, with its five chimneys and two water towers, in the background. The 90 mm gun has a blast deflector on the muzzle, but the gun barrel lacks a bore evacuator.

A Ford-produced T48 chassis is being maneuvered onto (or off) a transporter. Visible above the engine deck is the engine exhaust, with two rectangular ports on its rear facet. Early Ford T48s had two storage boxes on the right fender, with the rear one being slightly lower than the front one.

The 90 mm gun has not been mounted on this Ford-built T48, undergoing tests. The driver, wearing a white helmet and dark-rimmed goggles, is visible in his hatch, which has not yet been fitted with the swiveling hatch door.

Initially, Ford built its T48s at its Highland Park, Illinois, plant, but during production, assembly of T48s was moved to Ford's new Livonia, Michigan, plant. The T48s seen here are under construction at Livonia, in or before mid-August 1952. A T-shaped blast deflector is affixed to the muzzle of the tank in the foreground. The next tank in line is about to receive its turret.

The precursor of the M48 medium tanks was the T48, seen with its T48 90 mm gun set at maximum depression of –9 degrees in an Aberdeen Proving Ground photograph from April 1952. *Patton Museum*

Two attributes that the T48 did not share with the later M48A3 were its low rear deck and lack of box-shaped air cleaners on the fenders. The shape of the T48's rear hull was different from that of the M48A3, with a solid armor design and a flat, rather than raised, top edge. *Patton Museum*

This early-production T48 is identified by the small type of driver's hatch that could be opened only with the surrounding periscopes lowered. This small hatch also made it difficult for the driver to exit the tank when the turret was locked to the rear in the travel position. Other early features include the low-profile commander's hatch, the lack of a track-tensioning idler behind the last road wheel, and the absence of the exhaust deflector on the engine deck. *Patton Museum*

Due to a tremendous need for new tanks, production of the T48 was begun before final trials were complete on pilot models. Many small changes were incorporated into the early batches of the T48. The addition of an exhaust deflector on the upper deck ahead of the gun travel lock is one of the first external changes. This production tank undergoes fuel consumption tests at the Detroit Tank Arsenal in May 1953. The T48 was issued to troops in limited numbers and through time received the many upgrades of the M48. *TACOM LCMC History Office*

Following the production of 1,000 T48 tanks, the vehicle was standardized as the "Tank, 90 mm Gun, M48," on April 2, 1953. Here, an M48 performs a deepwater-fording experiment across Lake St. Clair for the Detroit Arsenal, on May 22, 1953. Two exhaust trunks, or stacks, were installed on the engine exhausts on the top of the rear deck. *TACOM LCMC History Office*

A T48 tank is being driven over a bridging device to assess its ability to cross trenches, at Aberdeen Proving Ground on April 12, 1952. The requirement was for the tank to cross a trench 96 inches wide, and the T48 was able to cross one that was 102 inches wide, but to do so it was necessary to remove the tow pintle to avoid breaking it.

The 90 mm gun of this M48 tank has been fitted with a T-shaped muzzle brake. To the rear of the muzzle brake is the bore evacuator, which drew gases out of the gun after it was fired, sparing the crew from noxious fumes. The dome-shaped objects jutting from the sides of the turret are the covers for the stereoscopic rangefinder. Oblong sighting openings are on the covers.

"T48" is stenciled in white on the side of the turret of a tank maneuvering along a dirt road. The white stenciling on the glacis is only partly legible, but it included "TEST OPERATION." *Kevin Emdee collection*

An M48 is ascending a steep grade, evidently as part of testing of the vehicle. The M48 could negotiate slopes up to 60 percent (31 degrees). Under high magnification, registration number 30173011 is visible on the forward part of the storage box on the right fender. What seems to be a tow cable stretches from the bow to the top of the incline. *Kevin Emdee collection*

Three M48 tanks are negotiating a muddy trail in a forest clearing. The belly of the lead tank is almost touching the ground. The 90 mm gun barrels of all three tanks have cylindrical blast deflectors on the muzzle ends. *Kevin Emdee collection*

The 90 mm gun of a T48 has just been fired, kicking up dust to the front of the tank. Stenciled in white on the side of the turret is "T/48." A conical flash suppressor is on the muzzle of the .50-caliber machine gun mounted on the cupola. *Kevin Emdee collection*

During a performance test or a training session, an M48 with its turret trained to the rear is negotiating a ravine. The registration number, 30173011, is stenciled on the storage box on the fender. The travel lock is taller than those often seen in photos of M48s, causing the 90 mm gun barrel to have a noticeably elevated position when resting on the lock. *Kevin Emdee collection*

With its internal fuel tanks with a capacity of 200 gallons of 80-octane gasoline, the M48 had a range of approximately 70 miles. To extend the range, some of the tanks were equipped with a jettisonable rack fabricated from tubes, to hold four 55-gallon steel fuel drums, more than doubling the tanks' stock fuel capacity. The curved structure to the front of the fuel drums would seem to be a deflector for the 90 mm gun barrel, when it was being aimed toward the rear. *Kevin Emdee collection*

The commander of the M48 tank could either remotely control and fire the .50-caliber machine gun on the cupola from inside the turret or operate it manually, as seen here. This vehicle bears US Army registration number (sometimes referred to as "USA number") 9A1899 on the side of the stowage box on the fender.

A .50-caliber gun mount on an M48 tank is shown with the .50-caliber machine gun dismounted. In the foreground is the left rangefinder cover.

Soldiers of the 145th Infantry Regiment catch a ride on an M48 tank as they advance toward the "enemy" during Exercise Flash Burn at Fort Bragg, North Carolina, on April 29, 1954. On the bow of the tank are markings for the sixth vehicle, B Company, 44th Tank Battalion, 82nd Airborne Division. On the turret is the number 16 inside a circle.

Two M48 tanks pause during a road march as part of an exercise. Both vehicles have a hastily applied camouflage scheme, possibly consisting of mud, over the Olive Drab base color. The markings on the fenders of the lead tank appear to pertain to Company B, 112th Cavalry Regiment, 49th (Lone Star) Armored Division. Note the two tubes emanating to the driver's left; these were dual exhausts for the individual personnel heaters for the driver and for the fighting compartment, a characteristic of the M48 and M48A1 tanks.

The layout of the M48 suspension includes five track return roller wheels per side and shock absorbers on the first two road-wheel stations. The exhaust pipes for the crew heater are visible just forward of the fender-mounted stowage box.

The flat engine deck and lack of the machine gun cupola make the M48 a very distinctive tank. The exhaust for the gasoline-fueled crew heater was mounted on the left side of the driver's hatch in these early-production tanks. The smooth contour of the large single piece of turret casting is shown to good effect from this angle. The turret design eliminated any forward shot traps except directly below the gun mount. The engine deck is fitted with the exhaust deflector ahead of the travel lock.

The layout of the suspension of the right side of an M48 is displayed, from the sprockets at the rear, to the five dual track-support rollers and six dual bogie-wheel assemblies, to the dual idler wheels at the front. The sprocket drums lacked the mud-relief holes of later models of the M48 series.

In a view of the right side of the turret of an M48 tank, toward the rear (*left*) is the stowage rack on the bustle and a holder for a 5-gallon liquid container. Along the turret is a grab rail, often used for securing knapsacks and gear. To the rear of the rail is a lifting lug, and on the fender is a stowage box for equipment.

The flat engine deck and the 28-inch-wide T97 track make the rear of an M48 look extremely wide and low. Early tanks had the smooth, rounded fenders front and rear. The raised boxlike projection in the center of the rear plate houses an infantry telephone. The two smaller projections above the towing points are removable access panels for the transmission. Note the mounting housings for the missing taillights for comparison to later models.

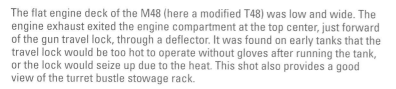

The flat engine deck of the M48 (here a modified T48) was low and wide. The engine exhaust exited the engine compartment at the top center, just forward of the gun travel lock, through a deflector. It was found on early tanks that the travel lock would be too hot to operate without gloves after running the tank, or the lock would seize up due to the heat. This shot also provides a good view of the turret bustle stowage rack.

In a view over the rear deck of an M48 tank, grab handles for the transmission-access grille doors are in the foreground. Farther forward is the travel lock for the 90 mm gun, with the engine exhausts (box-shaped objects with horizontal slots) visible on the deck below the turret bustle. The transmission oil filler cover is to the right of the centerline of the deck.

The turret of the T48 was a large single-piece casting, as was the outer gun shield for the T41 90 mm main gun. The T48 and early M48s are marked by the exhaust for the crew heater exiting on the left side of the driver's hatch. The early small-pattern hatch lid closed flush against the hull armor and disappears from view in this view. The purpose of the bracket on the turret roof is unknown and is not a factory fitting.

The dual exhaust pipes for the two personnel heaters of the M48 tank exit from the hull to the left of the driver's hatch and terminate above the outboard edge of the left fender. Also in view are details of the front fender bracket (*left foreground*), the left rangefinder cover, and, on the front of the turret, the bosses for fastening the gun-shield cover.

In this overhead view the bulge within the commander's hatch plate is visible. This bulge provided additional room for the commander to use the periscopes. Although this style of hatch was seen as a weakness of the early design, a similar design was used by the Israelis on their updated M48s and was later chosen to replace the M1 cupola on the M48A5. This was the final update program of US tanks in the 1980s. *Scott Taylor*

The early-style commander's hatch of the T48 and M48 is here traversed to the rear. It is missing the mount for the M2 .50-caliber Browning machine gun. The hatch assembly mounted four fixed periscopes for 360 degrees of vision. The hatch lid, when open, could be locked at 90 degrees to provide armored protection for the commander's back. *Scott Taylor*

The bow of the M48 tank had the characteristic bulged look that all future versions of the M48 family would share. The tank is equipped with T97 tracks, a double-pin, rubber, chevron-tread design with a width of 28 inches and a pitch (front-to-rear measurement) of 6.94 inches. The chevron treads are worn down on this example.

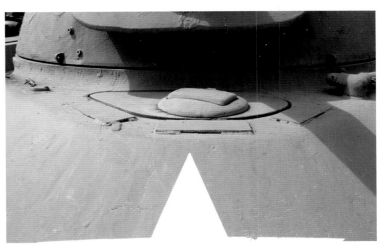

The driver's hatch door of the M48 was opened by slightly raising it and swiveling it to the right side. The driver was provided with three periscopes; the covers for the periscopes have been removed and blank plates welded over their openings. On the hatch door is a mount and lid assembly for installing an M24 infrared periscope. This style of hatch replaced a smaller version found on early-production T48 and M48 tanks, which also lacked the mount for the infrared periscope.

The headlight groups of the M48 tank had a bow-shaped brush guard. The right group, shown here, had, *left to right*, a service headlight, a blackout marker light, and a blackout service headlight. Missing from this vehicle is the horn, which was mounted above the blackout marker light.

The left headlight group of the M48 tank repeated the service headlight, blackout marker light, and blackout service headlight as found on the right side, and also included a blackout drive light above the blackout marker light.

By 1963 the Army had decided to go to Diesel-powered tanks, the M48A3 being chief among these. The M48A3s were produced at Anniston Army Depot and Red River Army Depot by converting M48A1 tanks. At about the same time, Rock Island Arsenal rebuilt M48 gasoline-powered tanks for foreign military assistance programs, including this tank about to be reconditioned for shipment to Libya. *Rock Island Arsenal Museum*

One of the first steps in the rebuild process was draining of lubricants from the powerplant and various gearboxes. The rear hull design of the gasoline powered tanks is clearly evident here. *Rock Island Arsenal Museum*

After complete disassembly, the hull was shot blasted to clean it up. Some M48 hulls were produced by single-piece castings, while other hulls were welded together from seven smaller castings. *Rock Island Arsenal Museum*

Large fixtures were used to hold the cleaned hulls securely in place as welders repaired damage and performed modifications during the rebuilding process. The large circular opening in the hull bottom nearest the camera is the driver's escape hatch. *Rock Island Arsenal Museum*

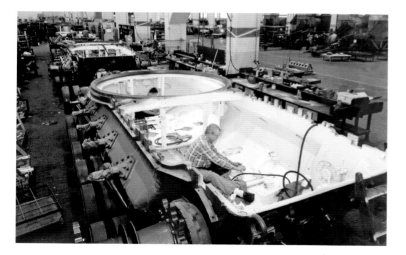

Reconditioned M48 hulls move down the line during the reassembly process. The cast armor hull and turret are among the most expensive components of a tank, and reuse of those components through rebuilding is an economical way of building "new" tanks. *Rock Island Arsenal Museum*

All members of the M48 family rode on torsion bar suspensions. The details of the suspension system show clearly in this photo of an M48 during rebuild. Shock absorbers were mounted on the first two and last road wheels, while the number and placement of track return support rollers varied from model to model. *Rock Island Arsenal Museum*

Turrets and guns were rebuilt on their own assembly lines. All members of the M48 family up until the M48A5 were armed with the 90 mm Gun M41 using an M87A1 mount. This mount provided +19° to -9° elevation, while the turret gave 360° traverse. *Rock Island Arsenal Museum*

The Achilles heel of the M48 was the gas-thirsty Continental AV-1790. With this powerplant the 200-gallon fuel tanks gave the M48 a range of only 70 miles. The Diesel powered M48A3 had a 385-gallon fuel capacity and a range of 300 miles. *Rock Island Arsenal Museum*

CHAPTER 2

M48A1

The "Tank, 90 mm Gun, M48A1" was basically an M48 tank with a large driver's hatch, with an M1 commander's cupola replacing the Chrysler-designed cupola. Developed by Aircraft Armaments, Inc., the M1 cupola was a fully rotating assembly with a fully enclosed .50-caliber machine gun. The commander fired the machine gun from inside the cupola, sighting through a T42 or M28 periscope in the cupola roof. The commander had all-around vision through the sight and five vision blocks on the cupola. *TACOM LCMC History Office*

The T48/M48 was equipped with a Chrysler-designed, low-profile commander's cupola featuring four periscopes. Mounted on the cupola was a .50-caliber machine gun that could be aimed and fired from inside the turret via a mechanical linkage. However, to reload the weapon or clear a jam, the commander had to open the cupola hatch and expose himself to possible enemy fire.

The firm Aircraft Armaments, Inc., developed a commander's cupola that featured a .50-caliber machine gun mounted inside the cupola; thus the commander could fire and reload the weapon without opening the cupola hatch. A T42(M28) periscopic sight atop the cupola was used to aim the weapon, and five vision blocks were installed in the sides of the cupola. The new cupola, known as the M1 cupola, was approved for use on production of M48

tanks in August 1953. By late 1954, over 3,200 T48/M48 tanks had been built, which included tanks with small and large driver's hatches, tanks with defective hulls, tanks with the Chrysler-designed cupola, and tanks with the Aircraft Armaments M1 cupola. To clarify things, on October 13, 1954, Ordnance Technical Committee Minutes 35619 laid down new nomenclature. Per this instruction, tanks with the small driver's hatch and the Chrysler cupola were M48. The tanks with smaller driver's hatches, Chrysler cupolas, and defective hulls were designated M48C. The large-hatch tanks had their Chrysler cupolas replaced with the M1 cupola and thereafter were redesignated the M48A1. Both the M48 and M48A1 were standardized, but the M48A1 was preferred for overseas deployment.

An M48A1, distinguishable by its five track-support rollers and the Aircraft Armaments Model 30 commander's cupola, is nearly complete at the Grand Blanc plant. *Grand Blanc Heritage Museum*

An M48A1 maneuvers through wildflowers on a testing ground at the Fisher Body Division's plant at Grand Blanc, Michigan. Numbers have been hand-painted on the cupola (323) and on the lower forward part of the turret (2816). Unpainted, bright-metal screws and washers abound on the fenders and fender supports. *Grand Blanc Heritage Museum*

The same M48A1 is observed from the right front on the testing ground at Grand Blanc. Painted on the right front of the glacis is the number V-2804. A muzzle brake is not installed on the 90 mm gun, and the muzzle and the bore evacuator are wrapped in tape. *Grand Blanc Heritage Museum*

As a solution to the relatively low range of the M48A1, the "Jettison Fuel Tank Kit M48A1" was developed. It was a tubular support frame with two inclined racks on top. Each rack held two 55-gallon gasoline drums. When the drums were emptied, they could be jettisoned. This view of the kit, as installed on the rear of a turretless chassis, was dated June 21, 1957.

The M48A1 jettison fuel tank kit is seen from the rear on the M48 chassis, showing the design of the tubular frame and inclined racks. A white measuring stick is propped up atop the tow pintle. Light-colored U-bolts were used to attach the bottom of the frame to large pad eyes, which were welded to the rear of the hull.

An unmounted M48A1 jettison fuel rack with four 55-gallon gasoline drums installed is viewed from the left front. Steel straps secured the drums on the racks. Fuel hoses are installed, with couplings for them being welded to the racks.

Four 55-gallon drums stenciled "GASOLINE" are lined up on the jettison fuel rack on an M48. When jettisoned, the drums would roll off to the sides. Above the center fuel drums is the muzzle brake of the 90 mm main gun, which is traversed to the rear; a dustcover is taped to the muzzle brake. *Rock Island Arsenal Museum*

An M48A1 tank, USA number 9A8002, rolls through Sprachbrücken, Federal Republic of Germany, during maneuvers in November 1963. This vehicle has markings for the 66th Armor Regiment, 2nd Armored Division, which was airlifted to Germany for these maneuvers. Mounted above the mantlet of the 90 mm gun is a Crouse-Hinds 18-inch searchlight.

During winter maneuvers, an M48A1 tank emerges from an M2 Bailey bridge. The fronts of the fenders have been cut back at an angle. Visible among the roughly applied whitewash camouflage on the turret is a large triangle with the number 12 faintly visible inside it.

M48A1, USA number 9A2340, conducts a winter exercise. Whitewash camouflage has been applied sparingly to the turret and the 90 mm gun. A triangular tactical symbol with the number 22 inside it is on the turret. On special racks to the rear of the hull are jettisonable fuel tanks, designed to increase the operating range of the tank.

Proceeding along Friedrichstrasse, yards away from the famous Checkpoint Charlie, a Cold War flash point at the boundary between West Berlin and East Berlin, this M48A1, USA number 9A6196, has a different type of mount for the 18-inch searchlight than the one seen earlier, featuring V-shaped holders fabricated from metal tubing. A dustcover is fitted over the machine gun shield of the commander's cupola. Bedrolls are strapped to the handrails on the turret. This vehicle is equipped with a dozer blade; it rides somewhat nose down because of the extra weight at the front.

Three M48A1 tanks are poised at Checkpoint Charlie during one of the "tank standoff" crises during the Cold War, including the tank seen on the previous page. Many details are visible on the nearest tank, including the T97 rubber chevron tracks, a bulldozer kit on the front of the tank, and the foundry mark for the Continental Foundry, Coraopolis, Pennsylvania (the letter "C" with a letter "P" inside it), to the right of the left-rear lifting eye. This vehicle has a large steel box secured with a retainer bar in lieu of the smaller external telephone box often found at that location.

An M48A1 tank is emplaced behind the Berlin Wall. Although this tank was woefully inadequate compared to the Soviet tanks of the late 1950s an early 1960s, the M48A1 often was the only tank of resort available to US forces until the more powerful M60 tank came online.

Yards away from the famous Checkpoint Charlie, M48A1s churn toward the newly made boundary between West Berlin and East Berlin in a substantial show of force. The nearest tank has the USA number 9A2960, while the far one has the number 9A3173.

This M48A1 was preserved in running condition at the Ropkey Armor Museum. The tank is very complete, even including the fabric cover over the main gun shield. This tank retains the early position and twin pipes for the crew heater exhaust. The addition of the M1 cupola is the major identifying external feature of the M48A1, many being converted from the M48s, with large driver's hatches. *Skip Warvel*

The M1 cupola and rangefinder blister can be seen in this right-side turret shot. The cover for the gunsight is seen atop the cupola. Spent shell casings and the disintegrating links from the ammunition belts were ejected through the opening at the bottom of the forward bolted cover. Note the smooth texture of the cast components.

The forward shield for the .50-caliber machine gun was also a casting. The clips and fittings around the shield's edges are for attaching a canvas dustcover. The barrel and cooling jacket are that of a standard air-cooled M2HB Browning .50-caliber machine gun.

The hatch assembly at the rear of the cupola was also a casting housing two armored glass blocks. The casting numbers and foundry mark are visible in the center of the hatch. The cupola housed a hundred-round ammunition box for the gun that interfered with space for the commander and also made it difficult to change belts.

The loader's hatch cover opened to the rear and was held in place with a locking clip. The interior of the hatch was padded with a sheet of rubber; the heavy latching assembly is visible. Opening the heavy lid was assisted by two large springs on the exterior.

The right-rear corner of the turret interior was the office of the commander. The device across the turret roof is the housing for the rangefinder drive. The commander would lay this device optically on the target and bring it into focus by using the two sights in the external blisters on each side of the turret. The device then computed the range to the target for the gunner. The glass blocks of the M1 cupola are seen above.

In a view of the right side of an M48A1 turret interior, the right side of the T46E1 stereoscopic rangefinder is to the left, with the opening to the cupola at the top. At the far left are the diopter scales and the interpupillary scales, which the commander had to calibrate to his own sight in order to be able to operate the rangefinder. Between those scales and the turret wall on the bottom part of the rangefinder are the range knob and the ballistic computer switch. The commander's intercom control box is to the right of the center of the photo, and his seat back is to the far right.

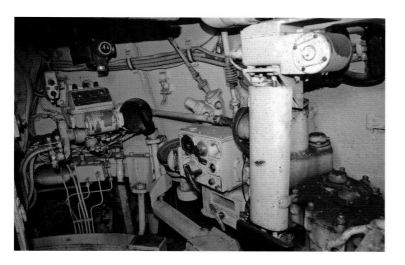

The gunner's station is in the right front of the turret. The gunner's controls include elevation and traverse controls on each side of the gun selector switches with indicator lights. Above this is the eyepiece for the M20 periscope. In the lower center of the photo is the T30 ballistic computer and azimuth indicator. To the right is the traversing mechanism with control for the commander.

Above the main gun is the linkage from the commander's rangefinder to the gunner's controls and periscope. The commander and gunner work in tandem to acquire a target as quickly as possible. The 90 mm gun's M87 mount used a concentric-style recoil device, which saved a tremendous amount of space within the turret.

The M87 gun mount seen from above, with the ballistic control linkage across the turret roof. The empty brackets are for the direct telescopic sight at the right of the gun, and for the coaxial mounted .30-caliber machine gun at left. The turret front was sealed from moisture and dust by a fabric bellows around the gun mount opening.

At the turret rear is mounted the communications equipment. The M48 series was equipped with a large variety of radio equipment throughout their service history, including units with air-to-ground capability. The radio was linked into the tank's internal system, which includes four intercom boxes for the crew.

The lower hull of the M48 series was originally designed to be cast as a single huge casting. The boatlike shape of the lower hull casting is evident here. To ease the load on foundries, a lower hull was developed that was made up from seven cast and rolled components welded together. The front fender extensions are missing from this tank and are seldom seen undamaged in service. *Skip Warvel*

The driver's hatch rose slightly and swung back to the right to open. This allowed it to clear the three fixed M27 periscopes that surrounded it, mounted within the hull. The center section of the hatch is a rotating mount that could carry the M24 infrared periscope for night driving. The periscope had to be removed from the hatch before opening.

The hull front was home to the driver's position. The steering wheel is seen at center, with the transmission selector lever on the steering stalk. The accelerator pedal is visible behind the steering wheel at the lower right. The light at the top center is the main engine-warning light. The knob to the left of the wheel is a hand throttle control. The cylinders on the floor at the right are part of the fire extinguisher system.

To the right of the driver, behind the fire extinguisher bottles, is the instrument panel. The pair of switches controls many electrical systems, from the headlights to the engine magnetos. The gauges are for fuel tanks and oil pressure. The center of the panel has a number of warning lights for fuel and oil pressure of the engine and transmission as well as the generator system.

Below the instrument panel in the lower right front of the hull is the control panel for the auxiliary generator. Gasoline-burning M48s used an auxiliary power supply to save running the engine to operate secondary systems on the tank while stopped. This saved wear and tear on the engine as well as fuel.

The missing rear fender extensions afford an excellent view of the final-drive housings at the lower hull rear. This tank has a single piece lower hull casting with the foundry marks and casting numbers to the right of the telephone box. The four bolts below the left-side lift ring on the turret are for mounting a fuel can rack. *Skip Warvel*

The rear portion of the engine deck is made up of two transmission-access doors. The large Continental twelve-cylinder engine was air-cooled. The deck incorporated an intricate system for the intake and exhaust of cooling air. The M48A1 was equipped with the CD850-4 cross-drive transmission, which was a development of the transmission first designed for the M46.

The engine exhaust exited the engine compartment at the top center. The engine deck was equipped with an exhaust deflector to split the flow of the hot exhaust around the gun travel lock. This made the travel lock less likely to seize up while traveling and easier to handle. Flat-profile lifting handles are attached to the edges of the various deck plates.

The first and second road-wheel stations on the M48A1 were equipped with shock absorbers. The torsion bars exited the lower hull through castings bolted to the hull side. The travel of each swing arm was limited by a volute spring bump stop. Note the detail of the linkage between the swing arm and shock on the first left-side road wheel.

CHAPTER 3
M48A2/M48A2C

With the T48E2 project, which commenced in early 1954, the raised rear deck that is a key feature of the post-M48A1 tanks came into being. This deck enclosed a radically new engine exhaust system comprising an insulated exhaust tunnel running over the engine and emitting exhaust gases through two grille doors at the rear of the hull. This redesigned exhaust system reduced the infrared signature of the tank, making it more difficult for the enemy to detect. The rear deck is noticeable in this photo of T48E2, USA number 9A-4174, dated April 27, 1955, showing the 90 mm gun fully elevated. *Patton Museum*

Fuel consumption, and the related limited range, plagued the naturally aspirated M48/M48A1 and was of concern to US Army strategists. A three-prong strategy was first considered to address this. Two of the prongs involved the use of the newly developed AVI-1790-8 fuel-injected engine; the engine itself was more fuel efficient, plus the outrigger oil coolers and their belt-driven fans of the AV-1790-5B and AV-1790-7 (used in the M48/M48A1) were replaced with a newly designed oil cooler mounted around the top of the engine, which utilized the main engine fan. The result was a more compact design, which allowed internal fuel storage to be increased from 200 to 380 gallons of gasoline, the space previously taken up by fans and coolers now containing fuel tanks. The third prong of the attack was a new transmission, the XT-1400, which was more efficient and less expensive.

The new transmission design reduced the ground clearance of the vehicle, which was strongly objected to during the testing of the vehicle, dubbed M48E1, at Fort Knox.

As a result, work was begun on the M48E2, which again featured the AVI-1790-8 coupled to a modified version of the CD-850 transmission. This engine and transmission installation required a redesign of the rear deck of the tank. It was also decided that the infrared signature of the vehicle should be reduced. The exhaust was no longer directed out the top of the louvered deck but instead was routed through two large louvered doors at the rear of the hull. Previous models had slanted rear armor plate at this location. The new deck and hull rear addressed both the cooling and infrared concerns. In the new configuration, fuel capacity was raised to 335 gallons, which gave the tank a range of about 160 miles.

In addition to the range and concealment concerns mentioned above, other problems were addressed as well. Due to suspension failures on the tanks, improvements were made in this area, including new spindle bearings, eliminating the second and fourth track return rollers, a new track-adjusting link, double bump springs on

The grille doors at the rear of the hull of the T48E2, as initially installed, are depicted. These had vertical, inward-angled louvers. The design of these doors would be changed during testing to incorporate diagonal, outward-pointing louvers. In a small recess at the rear of the top deck was the new travel lock. Farther forward on the solid center panel is marked "NON-BALLISTIC," indicating the panel is made of mild steel. To the sides of the solid center panel are air-intake grille doors. *Patton Museum*

the front road-wheel arms, and replacement of the hydraulic shock absorbers with friction snubbers on the two front and rear road wheels. The friction snubbers closely resembled hydraulic shock absorbers but relied on friction between a lining and piston, rather than the fluid, to dampen movement. The result is a longer-lived, more reliable suspension, albeit with a harsher ride.

Work was also undertaken to improve turret traverse and gun elevation control. To this point, an Oilgear system had been used, but after evaluating both a Minneapolis Honeywell amplidyne

system and a Cadillac Gage constant-pressure hydraulic system, the decision was made to use the latter.

On October 6, 1955, the Ordnance Committee standardized a new tank incorporating the improvements outlined above as the M48A2, and in December it was approved for production. Contracts were awarded to Chrysler's Delaware plant as well as to ALCO Products (formerly American Locomotive Company) to produce 2,328 of the new tanks.

Field use and further testing called for further modification to the design, including a new rangefinder. The troublesome M13A1 stereoscopic rangefinder was replaced by the M17 coincidence rangefinder, the small tension idler wheel introduced on the M48A1 was eliminated, and a larger-capacity bore evacuator was installed. On January 14, 1959, the Ordnance Committee designated vehicles with these improvements as M48A2C, and efforts were made to modify the 1,344 M48A2 tanks already completed to the new standard.

A driver is preparing to drive a completed M48A2 from the assembly line at ALCO's plant in Schenectady, New York. From here, the tank will be loaded onto a lowboy semitrailer for transport to the ALCO test center at nearby Niskayuna, New York. The bore evacuator and the ports of the rangefinder hoods have been taped over.

ALCO assembly-line workers and executives salute the first M48A2 tank to roll off the assembly line at the Schenectady plant. The M48A2 incorporated a number of improvements that were based on experience with the M48A1, including eliminating two track-support rollers on each side, resulting in three rollers, and redesigning the engine deck, which now had a pronounced hump.

Eleven turret assemblies for M48A2 tanks are lined up on the factory floor at ALCO in Schenectady. All but two of the turrets are on work stands with wheels, for moving along twin tracks on the floor. Numbers are chalked on the turrets: the first five tanks are numbered, from nearest to farthest, 47, 49, 50, 51, and 52.

Welders are working on M48A2 hull assemblies at ALCO, while three officials confer to the left. The engine compartments are painted white, with the power plants yet to be installed in them. Stacked in the middle background to the left are Hollywood mufflers.

Together, ALCO and Chrysler produced a total of 2,328 M48A2 tanks. This example was seen on the test course at Aberdeen Proving Ground on August 28, 1961. *TACOM LCMC History Office*

One design departure of the M48A2 from the M48A1 was the former's flat frontal plates on the fenders, reinforced with brackets referred to as outriggers, as opposed to the curved fronts of the fenders of the M48A1. The M48A2's front outriggers had a distinctive T shape toward their outboard ends. *Patton Museum*

The infrared signatures of the A2s and A2Cs were less than that of the earlier vehicles due to the redesigned grilles and louvers of the hull rear. Exhaust gases, which previously had exited just behind the turret, now traveled through a boxlike tunnel atop the engine deck before exiting the grilles at the rear of the tank. *Patton Museum*

M48A2, USA number 9B0041, is being driven on a test run at the factory. A portion of the humped rear deck is visible to the rear of the turret. The M48A2 retained the M1 cupola, although the .50-caliber machine gun is not mounted on this example. Like the M48A1, the M48A2 retained the M41 90 mm gun in the M87 mount. *TACOM LCMC History Office*

The rear grille doors of the M48A2, as developed during testing of the T48E2, are seen in this January 1957 photo. The louvers were tilted at a 22.5-degree angle and were designed to deflect exhaust gases outward and upward, thus reducing the amount of dust that was stirred up. Other changes included reducing the number of track-support rollers from five to three on each side. *Patton Museum*

A Patton tank is being lowered onto a flatcar at Newark Assembly Plant. Many details of the vehicle, and the one on the car in the background, are obscured by shadows and the stowed boxes, but the nearest vehicle appears to be an M48A2, on the basis of the presence of the track-tension idler below the sprocket, the flat mudguards, and curved mudguard supports on the rear, which are visible only under high magnification of the image. What appears to be a cover is affixed to the rear of the door-grilles, and the gun barrel lacks the blast deflector.

"TEST OPERATION" and a "50" bridge-classification symbol is on the glacis of an M48A2 at an unidentified facility. The series of pad eyes welded to the upper and lower parts of the bow were for mounting an appliqué armor kit, which featured a steel shell with a thick glass core. *Kevin Emdee collection*

Turret trained to the rear, this M48A2 with registration number 9B0302 displays the slightly humped engine deck, which incorporated an insulated exhaust tunnel, designed to reduce the infrared signature of the tank. "M-48A2" is stenciled on the side of the turret. *Kevin Emdee collection*

M48A2, registration number 9B0813, was equipped with an experimental suite of AGM-22A wire-guided antitank missiles. The AGM22A was the US version of the French SS.11 wire-guided antitank missile, and the installation seen here is similar to those on the French AMX-13 tank. The blue warheads indicate that these were inert training missiles. *Kevin Emdee collection*

Some M48A2C tanks, an improved version of the M48A2 whose visible distinguishing marks included the omission of the track-tensioning idlers below the sprockets, saw service in Vietnam. The ubiquitous rations boxes are stacked on the fenders and the turret of this M48A2C in the Republic of Vietnam. The nickname "Wild One III" is painted in white on the bore evacuator of the 90 mm gun. The USA number, 9B0311, is painted in white on the side of the storage box on the fender. *Chris Harlow*

Sgt. Loy M. Lee, commander of the M48A2C nicknamed "Willie," stands in the cupola behind a .50-caliber machine gun on a pintle mount atop the cupola, a common modification that gave the commander more exposure to enemy fire but greater control over the aiming of the machine gun. The tank and crew were assigned to Troop A, 4th Battalion, 4th Cavalry, 1st Infantry Brigade, and the photo dates to late August 1968. *NARA*

"Willie" was operating with an M113 ACAV personnel carrier on Highway 1 in late August 1968. Both vehicles were assigned to Troop A, 4th Battalion, 4th Cavalry, 1st Infantry Brigade.

"Willie" and an M113 ACAV of Troop A, 4th Battalion, 4th Cavalry, take up position along Highway 1, where they will provide guard duty through the coming night. Illegible writing is painted in pale yellow on the bore evacuator of the tank's main gun.

While most Pattons operated in Vietnam were the diesel-powered M48A3 variant, a few of the gasoline-fueled M48A2 versions were used following armor losses sustained repelling the 1968 Tet Offensive. This M48A2, with the 1st Battalion, 77th Armor Regiment, was photographed on January 6, 1969, supporting 1st Battalion, 5th Infantry Division (Mechanized), during Operation Fisher. *Patton Museum*

Both the identifying traits of the M48A2 are visible in this right-rear shot. The engine deck and hull rear are dominated by the new infrared-suppressing engine deck with a tunnel for the exhaust, and the return rollers are reduced to three per side. The new deck covered the central section of the upper hull, rerouting the exhaust to the rear to exit through the large rear grilles. The lack of the track-tensioning idlers further identifies this vehicle as an M48A2C. *Chun Hsu*

An M48A2C is viewed from the rear, showing the grille doors, below which are the taillights and their guards, the tow pintle, and three transmission-access panels: two square ones and, above the tow pintle, one round one. In addition to the omission of the track-tensioning idlers, the M48A2C featured a new M17C coincidence rangefinder to replace the troublesome stereoscopic rangefinder of the previous versions of the M48, a new M5A2 ballistic drive, and other changes. *Chun Hsu*

The new rear deck was flanked on each side by grilles for the intake of engine-cooling air. The exhaust still exited the engine compartment in the center top, but pipes and tubular mufflers routed the gases toward the rear of the hull. The infantry phone box has been relocated to the right-rear fender. Brackets on the fender are for securing the hand-operated fuel pump to pump fuel from 55-gallon drums into the tank's fuel cells. Similar brackets are found on the air cleaner boxes on the M48A3 and A5s. *Chun Hsu*

The left-side fender mounted a toolbox and a bracket for a suite of pioneer tools. The gun travel lock is relocated to the aft end of the engine deck. This vehicle is complete with the end panels of the fenders. The track-tensioning idler wheel is missing from behind the last road-wheel station on this tank. This detail changes with various upgrade programs of the M48 series. *Chun Hsu*

In the foreground in a view from the left rear of an M48A2C is the rear outrigger or fender support. Next to the left rear air-intake grille is the left fender stowage box, and the item just forward of that box is a pioneer tool rack. A triangular lifting ring is on the rear corner of the rear deck. *Chun Hsu*

The turret bustle was equipped with a blower ventilator fan housed below the dome at the left rear corner. This removed smoke and fumes from the turret interior when firing the main gun. The details of the loader's escape hatch include the two helper springs and the lock clasp on the turret roof. Note the smooth texture of the castings of this era, and the crest of General Steel Castings Corp. on the left turret surface. *Chun Hsu*

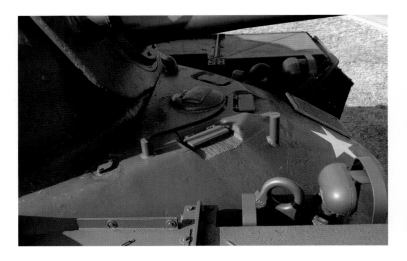

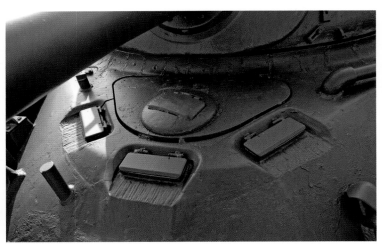

Details of the upper hull front include lifting lugs, external fire-extinguisher controls, the driver's hatch, driver's periscopes, and the exhaust for the crew heater. The white light and IR light headlight cluster, seen from the side, are a feature of the M48A2C tanks, as are the three support rollers and the new engine deck. The two rodlike projections are stops for holding the open driver's hatch. *Chun Hsu*

The driver's hatch, periscope covers, and hatch supports are seen from the left front. There are two hinges on each of the periscope covers. *Chun Hsu*

The M48A2C had a bore evacuator that was of larger capacity than that of the M48A2. To the front of the bore evacuator is the muzzle brake, a single-baffle design. The purpose of a muzzle brake is to retard the force of recoil of the gun. *Chun Hsu*

The muzzle brake is viewed from below. The side ports of the brake directed gas from the firing of a round to the sides and slightly to the front, creating a counterforce to the recoil of the gun. Allowing the gases to jet from the sides of the muzzle brake, rather than from the top and bottom, also had the effect of reducing the amount of dust stirred up when firing. *Chun Hsu*

As seen in an overall view of the right side of an M48A2C, noticeable hallmarks of this version included three track-support rollers, the absence of the track-tensioning idler between the rear bogie wheel and the sprocket, and the humped rear deck. *Chun Hsu*

M48 General Data					
Model	**M48**	**M48A1**	**M48A2C**	**M48A3**	**M48A5**
Weight*	99,000	104,000	105,000	107,000	108,000
Length	332.5	343.7	342	341.7	366.4
Width	148	143	143	143	143
Height	107.5	123.3	121.6	129.3	120.5
Crew	4	4	4	4	4
Armament	90 mm M41 .50 cal. M2 HB .30 cal. M1919A4E1 coaxial	90 mm M41 .50 cal. M2 HB .30 cal. M1919A4E1 coaxial	90 mm M41 .50 cal. M2 HB 7.62 mm M73 coaxial	90 mm M41 .50 cal. M2 HB 7.62 mm M73 coaxial	105 mm M68 2 × 7.62 mm M60D on turret top, 7.62 mm M219 coaxial
Maximum speed	26 mph	26 mph	30 mph	30 mph	30 mph
Fuel capacity	200 gal.	200 gal.	335 gal.	385 gal.	385 gal.
Range	70 miles	70 miles	160 miles	300 miles	300 miles
Electrical	24 V negative	24 V negative	24 V negative	24 V negative	24 V negative
Fuel	gasoline	gasoline	gasoline	diesel	diesel
Turning radius	pivot	pivot	pivot	pivot	pivot

Note: Overall dimensions listed in inches. Measure with main gun facing forward, and antiaircraft machine gun mounted.
* Fighting weight, in pounds.

CHAPTER 4
Flame Tanks

During World War II, the US Marine Corps found an effective way to advance flamethrowers into intensive battle zones, while protecting the crews, by mounting flamethrowers on M3A1 Stuart and M4 Sherman tanks. In the early 1950s, this concept was extended to the new M48 tanks. The US Army Chemical Corps designed a prototype for the Marine Corps, designated the T67, which was tested at Aberdeen Proving Ground under Project No. TT2-757/B. The vehicle is seen in this and the following three photos during evaluations at Aberdeen on November 5, 1953. Marked on the turret is "U.S. ARMY CML. [CHEMICAL] CORPS." *Chun Hsu*

During World War II and, to a lesser extent, in Korea, the US military, and especially the US Marines, used flamethrower armed tanks to their advantage in particularly treacherous areas. Both terrifying and deadly, flame tanks are able to flush out enemy troops from hidden and well-fortified positions.

It is not surprising, then, that such a tank based on the Patton 48 would be desired by the Marine Corps, which had last fielded flame tanks based on the venerable Sherman. On October 13, 1954, the Ordnance Committee (which was tasked with developing vehicles not only for the Army, but the USMC as well) classified the M7-6 as "Standard" and as a component of the flamethrower tank T67, which was to be based on the M48. Developed at the behest of the US Army Chemical Corps, the M7-6 consisted of the M7 fuel and pressure unit coupled to the M6 flame gun. The flame gun system with turret was designated "Flame Thrower Turret T7."

Mounting this turret, the tank had only a three-man crew, since no loader was needed, but the driver, commander, and gunner sat in their normal positions.

The flame gun was designed to resemble the normal 90 mm gun, and a .30-caliber coaxial machine gun was mounted to the right of the main weapon. The former loader's hatch was obstructed by fueling and charging controls for the flamethrower.

Following testing by the Marine Corps, procurement was initiated on fifty-six T67 flame tanks based on the M48A1. In addition, seventeen T7 flamethrower turrets were procured. These turrets were used to replace turrets on M48A1 gun tanks, and the T67 was updated to M48A1 standard. As a result, the Corps had an inventory of seventy-four T67 flame tanks. On June 1, 1955, OTCM action 35901 standardized the T67 as the "Flame Thrower Tank M67," and the T7 turret as the "Flame Thrower Tank Turret

M1." Chrysler produced a conversion kit, designated T-89, which could be used to convert a gun tank to flamethrower tank in a period of eight hours, including replacing the main gun with the faux cannon flame projector.

After the M48A2 was introduced, so too was the M67A1, which was based on the fuel-injected vehicle and utilized the M7A1-6 flamethrower. The improved vehicle used the Cadillac Gage constant-pressure hydraulic control system. The gunner used a XM30 periscopic sight with a 48-degree field of view and ×1.5 magnification. Chrysler was contracted to produce thirty-five of the vehicles at their Delaware plant in 1955–56. The M67A1 was classified as "Standardized" by OTCM 36947 on January 8, 1959, and was the only variant of Patton 48–based flamethrower tank used by the US Army.

As the Marine Corps upgraded their tank fleet to the diesel-powered M48A3, they desired that their flamethrower tanks receive a similar upgrade. In late 1961, funding was provided to convert thirty-five of the USMC M67 tanks to incorporate the features of the M48A3. The pilot, designated M67E1 by OTCM 37966 on February 1, 1962, was completed by Detroit Arsenal. The vehicle was subsequently standardized as the "Full Tracked Combat Tank, Flame Thrower, M67A2" on June 25, 1962. The flame gun of all three of the M67 variants had an elevation range of +45 degrees to –12 degrees and could fire the thickened fuel up to 280 yards. Thereafter, seventy-three of the M67A2 flame tanks were produced alongside the M48A3s being converted at Red River and Anniston in 1963–64.

It was these flame tanks that the Marines used so effectively in Vietnam. While effective and without equal, public sentiment in the US turned against flame weapons, and all variants of the M67 were withdrawn from service in 1974–75.

The flame gun of the T67 was mounted in the turret and fired through a dummy gun tube that resembled a beefier version of the barrel of the 90 mm gun of the M48. To support this illusion, the dummy gun tube of the T67 was equipped with a fake bore extractor and muzzle brake.

The T67 is observed from the left rear, with the turret and flamethrower facing the front. The turret for the T67 was designated the "Flame Thrower Tank Turret M1." The flamethrower in the prototype T67 was designated the E28-30R1, which included the experimental E28 fuel and pressure system, and the 30R1 flame gun. This weapon later was standardized as the M7-6 mechanized flamethrower ("M7" was the fuel and pressure component, and "6" represented the M6 flame gun). Later, there was an improved version, the M7A1-6.

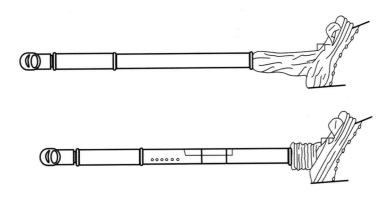

The T67 is seen from the front, in a final photo from Aberdeen Proving Ground on November 5, 1953. The brush guards for the headlight arrays were modified by flattening their tops, to allow the dummy gun tube to clear them when fully depressed. The turret traversed 360 degrees, and the flamethrower had an elevation of +45 to –12 degrees.

The standard barrel of the 90 mm gun of the M48 tank, *top*, is compared with the dummy gun tube of the T67/M67 flamethrower tank, below it. Features unique to the dummy tube include the dummy muzzle brake and bore extractor, perforations on the side of the shroud, and the access panel on the top of the shroud. On the bottom, the standard brush guard of the M48, with its rounded top (*left*) is compared with the brush guard of the T67/M67, with a flattened top.

A T67 is viewed from the left, with its dummy gun tube at a few degrees of elevation. Serial number 723 is in raised numerals on the lower part of the turret. The dummy gun tube was wider in diameter than the 90 mm barrel of the M48, and 21 inches shorter than the 90 mm gun barrel. The shroud was perforated, to allow combustion air to enter. A drip shield was on the bottom of the shroud, and there was an access panel on the center of the barrel for the ignition system. *Chun Hsu*

This T67, US Army registration number 9A6358, was equipped with a dozer blade, a searchlight atop the turret, headlights modified to clear the top of the dozer, and a portable fire extinguisher near the front of the right fender. *Chun Hsu*

A T67 marked "U.S. ARMY 7" on the storage box on the fender is armed with fixed .30-caliber machine guns in armored boxes on the fenders. These boxes are stenciled, "XOX BALLISTIC STEEL." Although the Marine Corps was the principal user of the T67/M67 flamethrower tanks, for a brief period the Army used a small number of vehicles designated M67A1. *Chun Hsu*

A US Army M67A1 flamethrower tank, registration number 9B2956, fires a stream of flame during a demonstration for students at the Dorrets Run Tank Range, at Fort Knox, Kentucky, on June 23, 1961. Painted on the turret is the nickname "RONSON," undoubtedly a reference to the Ronson flamethrower, developed by the British in World War II and used by the Canadian army and the US Marine Corps during that conflict. *Steve Zaloga*

Once the M48A2 tank was available, an improved version of flamethrower tank, the M67A1, was produced for the US Army on the basis of that chassis. At the heart of the M67A1 was the M7A1-6 flamethrower, comprising the M7 fuel and pressure system and the M6 flame gun.

Whereas the M67 flamethrower tank had the Chrysler commander's cupola, the M67A1 had the M1 cupola. Chrysler built a total of thirty-five M67A1s at the Newark, Delaware, plant from 1955 to 1956. Fuel for the flamethrower was stored in tanks in the turret. The M67A1 featured the Cadillac Gage constant-pressure hydraulic turret-control system.

The M6 flame gun on the M67A1 flamethrower tank was housed in a shroud disguised to look like a 90 mm gun, complete with fake bore evacuator and muzzle brake. However, the shroud was shorter and of slightly thicker diameter than the real 90 mm gun.

On the bottom half of the flamethrower shroud, to the rear of the fake bore evacuator, are perforations to admit air for combustion purposes. On top of the shroud is a form-fitting sheet-metal cover that permitted access to the ignition system.

The shroud of the flamethrower of an M67A1 flamethrower tank is seen from the left side, showing the ignition-system access cover and the dented, bogus bore evacuator.

The redundant muzzle brake, intended to disguise the flamethrower as a 90 mm gun, is viewed from the front. Unless a sharp-eyed enemy observer discerned that the "gun" actually was a flamethrower before it was too late, but for the mantlet, there was nothing else on the exterior of the vehicle that would betray it as a flamethrower tank.

The gun shield of the M67A1 flamethrower tank included a horizontally split ring where the flamethrower shroud met the shield, whereas the M48A2 tank had a solid ring at that position. Like the M48A2, the M67A1 had a .30-caliber coaxial machine gun protruding through the left side of the gun shield.

Although the right side of the gun shield of the M67A1 flamethrower tank retained the direct-sight aperture, the gunner actually aimed the flamethrower by sighting through an XM30 periscopic sight mounted in the turret roof, with magnification of ×1.5 and a 48-degree field of vision.

From the side, the turret of the M67A1 flamethrower tank appeared like that of any standard M48A2 tank. On the turret roof next to the .50-caliber machine gun barrel is the guard for the gunner's XM30 periscopic sight.

The M67A1 flamethrower tank was not produced in sufficient numbers to be influential. It was not the last flamethrower tank that would be based on the M48 family of chassis; in the early 1960s, the M48A3-based M67A2 would be produced and later would see service in Vietnam.

CHAPTER 5
M48A3

Under the M48A1E1 project, a 105 mm main weapon and a diesel power plant were installed and other improvements were made, but then ammunition costs caused that project to be aborted. Two of the six M48A1E1 vehicles were rearmed with 90 mm guns while other E1 improvements were retained, resulting in the M48A1E2 shown here. These two became the pilots of the M48A3 program.

By the late 1950s, the US Army and Chrysler were hard at work developing a successor vehicle, the M60. This coincided with the decision to adopt diesel as the new standard fuel for tanks. Tests conducted with the experimental diesel-powered M48A2E1 showed that the new fuel offered superior economy and far less fire/explosion risk than did the previously used gasoline.

Once the decision was reached to place the diesel-powered M60 in production, the Army looked at retrofitting the power plant from that tank, featuring the Continental AVDS-1790-2A twelve-cylinder engine, into the M48 family.

Along with the engine and CD-850-6A transmission, the rear deck and grille doors from the M60 were fitted to the M48A1. At the same time, the 105 mm main gun of the M60 was also installed in the tank, resulting in a vehicle referred to as the M48A1E1. Six pilots were produced.

In early 1961 the decision was made for the Army depot system to remanufacture 600 M48A1 tanks to these standards. However, the Army had vast stocks of 90 mm ammunition on hand, and there were budget concerns with regard to procuring sufficient additional 105 mm ammunition for the remanufactured tanks. Two of the M48A1E1s were rearmed, reverting to 90 mm guns, and were redesignated M48A1E2. These became the pilots for the next

generation of tank, the M48A3, which in time would be the primary medium tank used by US forces in Vietnam. The pilots could be distinguished from the production tanks by having three return rollers as opposed to the five found on production M48A3s.

During fiscal year 1962, Anniston and Red River Army Depots initiated a program of converting M48A1 tanks to M48A3 configuration. The change in power plant caused new air filter boxes to be mounted on the fenders. These filter boxes are the easiest way to tell a diesel-powered M48A3 from the earlier gasoline-fuel-injected M48A2. The conversion also involved the removal of the track tension idler. There were also several internal changes, including the installation of the fuel-burning personnel heater used in the M60, which required a rerouting of the heater exhaust. The first production conversions were completed in 1963, and by late 1964 about 600 M48A1s had been converted for the Army, and 419 more for the Marine Corps.

By the mid-1960s, the war in Vietnam was requiring additional armored assets, and the workload on the Army depot system was increasing as additional materiel of all types were required to sustain US troops.

To meet the demand for additional M48A3s, the Army turned to Bowen-McLaughlin-York (BMY), of York, Pennsylvania, awarding the firm a contract on April 14, 1967, to convert an additional 578

Engine Data: Gasoline					
Engine make/model	Number/arrangement of cylinders	Cubic-inch displacement	Horsepower	Torque	Governed speed (rpm)
Continental AVDS-1790-2	90-degree V-12	1,791	750 @ 2,400	1,710 @ 1,800	2,400
Engine Data: Diesel					
Continental AVSI-1790-5B, -7, -7B, -7C, -8	90-degree V-12	1,791.75	810 @ 2,800 rpm	1,560 @ 2,400 rpm	2,800

M48A3 **65**

M48A1 tanks to M48A3 configuration. However, these tanks differed from the depot-converted tanks of fiscal year 1962, and to distinguish the types the BMY-rebuilt tanks were referred to as M48A3 (Mod B).

Internally, the driver's controls were taken over from the M60A1, the rear grille doors and taillight guards were made more robust, and infrared fire control was provided for the gunner. Externally, these tanks were readily identified by the G305 riser package installed between the turret roof and the M1 cupola. This ring included nine vision blocks, and its installation beneath the commander's cupola improved his view as well as increasing headroom inside the cupola. Increasing headspace even more was a newly designed hatch for the cupola, which was bulged to accommodate the combat vehicle crewman's helmet. Because of the vision blocks in the riser ring, a vision block was not needed in the new hatch. In time, the G305 package was retrofitted to earlier M48A3s, and when that program had run its course the use of the Mod B designation was stopped.

The 3rd Platoon, Company B, 3rd Marine Tank Battalion, was the first US unit to arrive in Vietnam with tanks, bringing in M48A3s in March 1965. They were followed by more Marine

The installation of a diesel power plant was the result of a June 1958 change in policy, such that diesel could be used as the primary fuel for combat vehicles if such a fuel would contribute significantly to fuel economy. Continental quickly responded by developing a diesel version of its V-12 tank engine, which when fitted to the Patton 48 resulted in 60 percent improvement in fuel economy, with corresponding increase in range. This diesel power plant was chosen for the forthcoming M60, and in turn the decision was made to retrofit the M60 engine/transmission combination to older M48A1s, resulting in the "new" tank—model M48A3.

Like the standard M48A3, the M48A3 Model B had five return rollers per side, but these later tanks differed in details such as lighting and telephone systems, details of the rear grille doors, and, most obviously, the spacer ring between cupola and turret. These vehicles also had an enlarged cupola hatch. All these changes were ultimately made to earlier M48A3s as well, and the Model B designation was dropped. The machine gun deflector is visible on the turret of this M48A3 (Model B). The deflector prevented the cupola-mounted machine gun from firing into the back of the searchlight (not fitted in this photo).

tankers, and in October 1965 the First Squadron, 4th Cavalry, 1st Infantry Division, became the first US Army tank unit in Vietnam. Interestingly, Gen. George Patton's son, also George Patton, would command the 11th Armored Cavalry Regiment in Vietnam, a unit whose expert use of the tank added considerably to its fame.

In addition to the M48A3, the Marines brought with them the M67A2, which was a flame-throwing tank based on the M48A3, and a vehicle that was considerably feared by the Vietcong (VC). In July 1971, the M48A3 began to be supplied to the Army of Republic of Vietnam (ARVN; US ally South Vietnam), which used its 190 Pattons valiantly and effectively until the very end.

Although many had panned the use of the 52-ton Patton in Vietnam prior to its deployment, field experience proved the vehicle to be a tremendous asset. As seen in this volume, the M48A3 was valued for its thick armor, which protected the crew from deadly Vietcong mines. Its shear mass allowed it to plow through thick jungle vegetation.

Remarkably, in Vietnam the M48A3 was even attached to airmobile divisions. After frequent uncomfortable encounters with VC-fortified villages on the plains of Binh Dinh, the First Cavalry requested a tank company. This was furnished by 1st Battalion, 69th Armor, 4th Division, based in Pleiku. The tactic used was for one platoon of six to eight tanks to support an infantry battalion and crush the enemy.

Resupply was always a headache for tank operations in Vietnam. Often during the course of a heated battle, a tank would exhaust its basic load of sixty-two rounds of main gun ammunition and 2,000 rounds of .50-caliber. Accordingly, basic loads of tank ammunition were preslung for helicopter delivery and staged at nearby fire support bases prior to assault operations. Tanks could then be resupplied without recourse to slower, perhaps mobility-impaired, trucks.

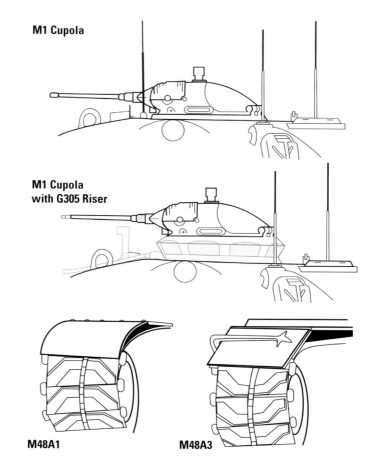

M1 Cupola

M1 Cupola with G305 Riser

M48A1   **M48A3**

From the front, the distinguishing characteristics between the M48A1 and M48A3 are harder to identify, with the most obvious difference being in the style of fender.

Landing craft *LCU-1476* from USS *Vancouver* (LPD-2) approaches Red Beach 2 to disgorge its load of Marine M48A3s on March 8, 1965. These men and other elements of the 9th Marine Expeditionary Brigade were part of the USMC force sent to secure the Da Nang airport and its surrounding area, which was the first major deployment of the USMC in the Vietnamese conflict. *USMC*

In the scrub some distance from the Da Nang Air Base, the commanding officer (*pointing*) of A Company, 3rd Tank Battalion, 9th MEB, gives instructions to his tank commanders on the impact area of a planned firing exercise on May 1, 1965. At this point, there was not a specifically designed role for Marine armor, and these types of exercises were essential to maintain a high state of readiness. *USMC*

After moving into position for the firing exercise, Marines of A Company, 3rd Tank Battalion, unload ammo from one M48A3 in order that it is distributed to the rest of the tanks. A clean tarp has been carefully laid on the ground to keep the rounds free of dirt, which could cause issues during the firing process. *USMC*

An M67A2 flame tank of B Company, 3rd Tank Battalion, guards the perimeter near Hoa Long village in 1965. This scene illustrates one of the biggest maintenance headaches for Marine tankers deployed in the coastal areas of Vietnam: fine sand. It was a constant source of aggravation, working its way into all areas of the suspension and tracks. Drive sprockets, which were normally reversed twice a year, were sometimes reversed daily to even wear. *USMC*

Infantry troops are taking advantage of an M48A3 as a battle taxi during Operation Lincoln south of Pleiku on March 27, 1966. The tank bears the markings for Company B, 69th Armor Regiment, 25th Infantry Division. The two white barrel rings indicate the company to which it was assigned—two stripes symbolize B Company. The tank carries its full complement of fenders, which are undamaged, indicative of its recent arrival in Vietnam. The driver is in the head's-up position and is wearing a CVC (combat vehicle crewman) helmet with built-in headphones and microphone. *NARA*

In the early part of the US presence in Vietnam, Marine armor was still frequently called upon to provide base and perimeter security, as is the case with the M48A3 standing watch over Marine Aircraft Group 36 at Ky Ha on November 18, 1966. The original caption points out that the individual in the commander's hatch is actually an aviator. This M48A3 lacks the distinctive round vision block beneath the cupola of the Model B and also mounts the earlier, circular Crouse-Hinds searchlight. A deepwater-wading snorkel has been stowed on the right side of the turret.

An M48A3 is being hoisted from SS *American Robin* at the Port of Saigon on September 15, 1966, and is about to join other M48A3s on a barge below, for transport to a dock. These tanks were assigned to the 11th Armored Cavalry Regiment and soon would be stationed at Long Binh. Crates with on-vehicle material parts are packed on the tanks. *NARA*

Mounted above the gun on many of the M48A3s operating in Vietnam was an AN/VSS-1 xenon searchlight, such as this one being cleaned on a tank from "D" Company, 1st Squadron, 11th Armored Calvary Regiment, in Long Binh on October 23, 1966.

A Marine Corps M67A2 is shown here in January 1966 burning the fields near the 1st Battalion, 3rd Regiment, command post in order to deprive the enemy of cover during possible attacks.

A Marine Corps M67 of the 1st Tank Battalion burns a VC area near Binh Son in the Quang Binh Province on October 5, 1966, as part of Operation Dozer. *Patton Museum*

A Patton moves quickly through an old rubber plantation near Xuân Lộc during a search-and-destroy mission in January 1967. One rear fender has been crumpled, and the other is largely missing from this vehicle with G Troop, 2nd Squadron, 11th Armored Cavalry Regiment.

This tank from the 3rd Marine Tank Battalion, shown in Dong Ha, is equipped with the early-style 18-inch Crouse-Hinds searchlight. The driver's periscopes were in the raised position when this photo was taken on March 2, 1967.

An M48A3 from C Company, 2nd Battalion, 34th Armored Regiment, waits for mines to be cleared on March 19, 1967.

A pair of spare road wheels are stowed on the fenders of this M48A3 from C Company, 2nd Battalion, 34th Armor Regiment, which lacks the spotlight above the main gun.

Canister, or "beehive," rounds were used extensively in Vietnam, as seen here. This 34th Armored Regiment Patton fires such a round into the vegetation alongside the road during a convoy operation on March 19, 1967.

Three M48A3s storm through Tây Ninh Province with machine guns blazing during Operation Junction City on March 19, 1967. The eighty-two-day operation, supported by armor, was the largest US airborne operation since World War II.

The dense jungles of Vietnam led many to believe that the terrain was unsuited to tank operations—but the need for heavy mobile fire support forced this idea to be challenged. This Patton from A Company, 1st Battalion, 69th Armor Regiment, is taking part in Operation Pershing near Truong Lin, Bình Định Province, northeast of An Khê, in June 1967. The Vietnamese stenciling on the turret side warns Vietnamese drivers to let the tanks pass when they were escorting convoys or moving on roads.

The North Vietnamese had only limited armored assets—primarily Soviet-built APCs. The M48 family, with its thick armor and powerful gun, could easily best any other armored vehicle encountered and make short work of most gun emplacements as well. This Patton, A12, A Company, 1-69 Armor, is involved in Operation Pershing about 90 kilometers northeast of An Khê.

When a US military vehicle was damaged or knocked out by the enemy, every effort was made to recover the vehicle and repair or salvage it. Here, a heavily damaged US Army M48A3 tank rests along with other vehicles at the base of the 218th Collection, Classification, and Salvage Company at Long Binh on June 14, 1967. Damage includes two rocket-propelled grenade (RPG) penetrations to the turret, a wracked muzzle brake, a ripped-off gun shield dustcover, and ripped fenders and stowage boxes. The many missing suspension components are likely the result of cannibalization to keep other vehicles in the field.

A landing craft, utility (LCU), moving a 3rd Tank Battalion tank up the Dong Ha River for unloading on July 6, 1967. Occasionally, Marine tankers would raise their M48s on landing craft by using large timbers. This would allow them to fire over the sides of the craft and create an ad hoc gunboat. This may be the case here, since the top of the track return run is visible. *USMC*

Marines of B Company, 1st Battalion, 4th Marines, and the tanks of the 3rd Tank Battalion team up together during Operation Hickory II on July 15, 1967. This operation also utilized SLF A and the 2nd Battalion, 3rd Marines. This was the first large search-and-destroy mission into the area south of the DMZ, in order to sweep and clear the area of enemy fortifications and mortar and artillery positions. Marine armor was essential for this task in providing fire support for the infantry.

This Marine M48A3 is equipped with the more common AN/VSS-1 xenon searchlight. An improvised shelter has been installed over the commander's cupola as protection against rain. The shelter would dangerously restrict vision while operating in the field, but this Patton and the Ontos visible in the background were defending the Khe Sanh perimeter when photographed on November 26, 1967. *Patton Museum*

This M48A3 tank attached to Charlie Company, 1st Marine Tank Battalion, was patrolling a beach in 1968. The "FY 67 3E" markings on the right-front fender indicate that this tank underwent third-echelon maintenance during fiscal year 1967. Cases of rations are stacked on both fenders. *Patton Museum*

Vietnamese civilians go about their business while the crew of an M48A3 is on the alert for enemy activity on February 1, 1968. The USA number on the fender storage box is 9A6730 (or possibly 9A6780). Spare tracks, ammo boxes, liquid containers, and even a pair of boots are stowed on the side of the turret.

This M48A3, dubbed "The Original Flower Children," rolls into the imperial walled city of Huế on February 12, 1968. The tankers are supporting the 1st Battalion, 5th Marines, during the bloody contest for the city. Like most tankers, the crew of this vehicle has strapped a range of gear to the outside of their vehicle. *Marine Corps Historical Center*

This M48A3 Model B was photographed in the city of Hue on the morning of Friday, February 2, 1968. This is undoubtedly a tank of A Company of the 3rd Marine Tank Battalion, which was part of the small relief force sent into Hue on January 31 to relieve the embattled MACV compound on the south side of the city. The convoy was met with heavy fire as they crossed the Phu Cam Canal, as indicated by the impact marks seen here on the glass blocks beneath the commander's cupola, and the gouges on the spare track blocks. About the time this photo was taken, North Vietnamese sappers dropped the Nguyen Hoang Bridge into the Perfume River, effectively cutting the city in half.

Refugees stream past an M67A2 flame tank on February 3, 1968. This tank was one of probably three flame tanks to see action in the coming battle. This photo was likely taken from one of the MACV buildings, with the gates of the Joan of Arc Church and School in the background. The church grounds would be infiltrated by NVA troops in the following days. Several sources cite the movement of civilian refuges that morning as they sought the relative safety of the MACV compound. Power lines lie on the sidewalk in the background, cut by enemy sapper teams.

Tank A51—the Alpha Company commander's ride—moves through Huế on February 12, 1968. An M60 machine gun team takes shelter beside the bulk of the M48A3 on the ground. During the fighting in the Imperial City, the tankers and infantrymen relied on each other for mutual protection. The gun tube sports the name "Mad Harlot," and there are two kill marks on the turret side just forward of the coincidence rangefinder.

Marines of the 1st Battalion, 5th Marines, and an M48A3 with the call sign A51 advance beside the northwest wall of the Citadel in Hue on Monday, February 12, 1968. The 1/5 was fresh to the fighting, having arrived via truck convoy from Phu Loc just the previous afternoon. Even before their arrival, the decision had been made to commit them to the Citadel. Although the Army of the Republic of Vietnam (ARVN) had hoped to retake this historically valuable area without American help, the intense clashes of the preceding few days had ground the South Vietnamese units down past the point of combat effectiveness. The battle for the Marines would begin in earnest the next day.

"Chaplain's Worry" is the nickname painted on the bore evacuator of M48A3, USA number 9A8652, performing security duty on Route 13 south of Ben Cat, Republic of Vietnam, in May 1968. The spare track sections stored on the turret provided extra protection from RPGs and were available for repairs should the tank detonate a mine. A xenon searchlight is mounted, and a .50-caliber machine gun is on a pintle mount on top of the cupola. *Office of History, US Army Corps of Engineers*

"Mr. Magoo," an M48A3 tank dozer named after the popular cartoon character of the 1960s, crosses an AVLB (armored vehicle-launched bridge) over a crater in the pavement of Route 13 south of Lai Khe, Republic of Vietnam, in February 1968. Cartoon art is faintly visible on the turret, and a bundle of sticks on the turret obscure the white-painted nickname. *Office of History, US Army Corps of Engineers*

An M48A3 tank dozer nicknamed "Charlie Brown," complete with a likeness of the cartoon character, pauses during an operation on Route 79 southeast of Ben Cat in June 1968. A bogie-wheel assembly is carried on the turret. Note the crumpling of the fenders. To the rear of the vehicle is a GI who has leaned his handheld mine detector against the sprocket. *Office of History, US Army Corps of Engineers*

An ARVN M113 personnel carrier passes a US Army M48A3 on a road south of Ben Cat in August 1968. A round, yellow bridge classification marking is on the bow of the tank, adjacent to the national insignia. *Office of History, US Army Corps of Engineers*

"Claustrophobia" is stenciled in red and white on each side of the turret of this tank. On the rear of the turret are strapped extra boots and what appear to be two purloined 40 mm Bofors gun ammo boxes. Such boxes made ideal large, waterproof stowage containers. Ration cases are stacked on the engine deck, and ammo boxes cover the fenders. Lashed securely to the commander's cupola and resting on the stanchion on the turret side is a purloined thermos.

"Claustrophobia" leads a column of APCs through the Vietnamese countryside on April 16, 1968. In Vietnam, where the North Vietnamese and Vietcong forces had only minimal armor, the US military relied on tanks to provide mobile fire support for infantry and convoy operations. This situation was in contrast to the tank-versus-tank duels that were a hallmark of combat in World War II and Korea.

"Claustrophobia" at Fire Base Bastogne in April 1968 has a moderate amount of additional stowage, including an orange plastic cooler on the rear of the turret and what appears to be a slave starting cable wrapped around the headlight guards.

Marines riding atop an M48A3, christened "No Name," cover their ears as the 90 mm main gun fires during a road sweep southwest of Phu Bai on April 3, 1968. Although it was common to transport Marine infantry on board tanks, it was a hazardous practice. In Vietnam, like all wars, tanks tended to draw small-arms fire. Additionally, they were susceptible to mines. There are numerous incidents of multiple causalities among riding infantry as a result of mine detonations, even when the tank crews themselves were not seriously injured.

This 1st Tank Battalion tank hit an enemy antitank mine outside a nearby hamlet while in support of D Company, 1st Battalion, 7th Marine Regiment, on May 20, 1968. The crew is beginning the unenviable task of changing the damaged section of tracks, which can just be seen in the foreground. Other photos from the sequence show that at least one road wheel was also damaged and swapped out. This photo was taken during the opening phases of Operation Mameluke Thrust, 6 miles north of An Hoa. The operation ran from May 19 through October of that year, and in addition to USMC units, it also included the 1st Squadron, 9th Cavalry.

This M48A3 of A Troop, 1st Squadron, 1st Cavalry, Americal Division, became mired while trying to cross a ditch in the waterlogged area 15 kilometers northwest of Hill 29 on August 2, 1968. While most of Vietnam was suitable for armor operations, some mountains and marshes were major impediments. The crew has opened their rations while waiting for recovery.

Mud flies into the air after a C4 demolition charge is set off to clear some of the mud from beneath the mired tank. The weight of the Patton's armor was a double-edged sword. The lighter M113 likely would not have become mired here—and if it had, it would have been extricated by a heavy-lift helicopter. However, the M48's armor allowed charges to be used to clear mud, as here.

After the charge has broken the suction of the mud and cleared some of the soil from the tank's undercarriage, no fewer than six M113 armored personnel carriers form a daisy chain and prepare to give the mired tank a pull. Such operations were fatiguing both to the men and the equipment but were part and parcel of combat operations in Vietnam.

Diesel smoke boiling from the exhaust grilles, the roaring Continental AVDS-1790-2A of the Patton works in concert with the Detroit Diesel engines of the APCs as the tank pulls free from the mire.

Crewmen replace the track of this 4th Cavalry M48A3 in the mud outside Saigon in August 1968. Not only were the tracks vulnerable to mine blasts, but, like the tires of a car, they also had to be replaced periodically due to normal wear and tear. The searchlight cover on this tank carries the legend "COOL BUT CRUEL." *Patton Museum*

A number of mine clearance accessories were available for M48 tanks in Vietnam, including mine plows, which excavated mines and shoved them to the side, and mine rollers, which used the weight of the roller to detonate mines. Shown here is an M48A3 nicknamed "Bandit" that is equipped with a mine roller made from sheep's-foot-construction compactor rollers. *Office of History, US Army Corps of Engineers*

An M48A3 tank attached to the 2nd Battalion, 26th Marines, Special Landing Force, goes ashore during an amphibious training operation at Cua Viet. Taking no chances, the LCU has delivered the tank directly to the sand. The South China Sea was notoriously rough, and the swells often created craters and runnels in the sand close to shore. These had been the cause of several incidents where tanks had been drowned, resulting in extensive recovery operations. This M48A3 has its deepwater-wading snorkel installed—not a common sight in photos. *National Museum of the United States Marine Corps*

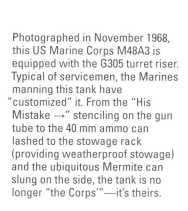

Photographed in November 1968, this US Marine Corps M48A3 is equipped with the G305 turret riser. Typical of servicemen, the Marines manning this tank have "customized" it. From the "His Mistake →" stenciling on the gun tube to the 40 mm ammo can lashed to the stowage rack (providing weatherproof stowage) and the ubiquitous Mermite can slung on the side, the tank is no longer "the Corps'"—it's theirs.

A particularly deadly variant of the Patton used exclusively by the Marine Corps in Vietnam was the M67A2 flame tank. The flame projector of the fearsome M67A2 vehicles was disguised as a standard cannon barrel, albeit slightly shorter. The flame gun had an elevation and depression range of +45 to –12 degrees—which was lower than the gun tank's barrel could depress. This difference required the tops of the light guards of the flame tanks to be flattened in order to provide clearance. This vehicle was photographed in Vietnam during 1968.

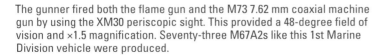

The gunner fired both the flame gun and the M73 7.62 mm coaxial machine gun by using the XM30 periscopic sight. This provided a 48-degree field of vision and ×1.5 magnification. Seventy-three M67A2s like this 1st Marine Division vehicle were produced.

Operating at a pressure of 300 psi, the M7A1-6 flame projector in the M67A2 could fire the thickened fuel up to 280 yards when using a ⅞-inch nozzle. The vehicle required no loader, so it had a three-man crew. The loader's hatch was used to access the flamethrower fueling and charging controls.

Three M48A3s go "jungle busting" in Vietnam. The 750-horsepower diesel engine combined with the 52-ton gross weight of the Patton meant that even the heaviest vegetation could simply be waded down. Pushing through heavy brush like this, even at low speeds, meant that all the "extra" gear that crews stowed on the outside of their vehicles had to be securely tied to the tank, or limbs would simply rake the material off into the jungle. *Patton Museum*

Other US tracked vehicles in Vietnam, specifically the M113 and M551, would have struggled to break this trail, risking engine overheating or immobilization. The VC sometimes rigged antipersonnel mines in the brush to target vehicle riders, and seasoned veterans rarely let their legs dangle over the sides or front of the vehicles. *Patton Museum*

The name "Hell's Henchmen" stenciled on the gun tubes of these M48A3s identifies them as belonging to H Troop, 2nd Squadron, 11th Armored Cavalry Regiment. At the center of the photo is the H Troop commander, Capt. Robert D. Hurt III. *Patton Museum*

Extra track links on the turret sides not only provided spares of this commonly needed item but also formed a sort of standoff protection against RPGs. If the RPG struck the spare links, the energy of the shaped-charge warhead would be dissipated before reaching the turret proper. *Patton Museum*

This M48A3 sports an elaborate, colorful paint job on the front of its hull. The forwardmost portion of the vehicle's fenders have been lost to the rigors of field operations. It is unclear exactly how the crew has secured their case of "Meal, Combat, Individual" to the side of the turret. The men are taking a break and enjoying cans of Pabst Blue Ribbon beer. *Chris Harlow*

"Wild One 4" was operated by the 919th Engineers. Engineers, charged with clearing brush, building bridges, and significantly ridding the roads of mines, were under constant threat of attack, and the tanks proved a significant asset to these troops. *Chris Harlow*

The crew of this 11th Armored Cavalry Regiment (ACR) M48A3 Mod B relax during a break. Protruding from the side of the turret, beneath the Mermite can, is the unused stowage bracket for the 2.2-kilowatt xenon searchlight. Other stowage on the vehicle includes a litter lying across the main-gun travel support and two jerry cans lashed across the jerry can bracket. *Patton Museum*

The Latin quote from Caesar painted on the spotlight cover—"VENI VIDI VICI"—was probably lost on the VC—and most US troops as well, but the translation, "I came, I saw, I conquered," typified the feelings of most Patton crewmen in Vietnam. *Don F. Pratt Museum*

The crew of this M48A3 doing perimeter defense work at a fire support base has rigged shelter halves as sunshades over the commander's cupola and on the ground behind the vehicle. Concertina wire is stowed on the rear grilles, and the rear fenders are covered with jerry cans and ration cases. *Don F. Pratt Museum*

Troopers from the 101st Airborne Division hitch a ride on an M48A3, the men and their gear completely obscuring the turret and engine deck. *Don F. Pratt Museum*

Loaded with men, extra jerry cans, ration cases, and ammo boxes, this M48A3 probably well exceeds the design weight of 107,000 pounds. At the rated weight, the M48A3 exerted 12.1 psi ground pressure, the weight being distributed along seventy-nine 28-inch-wide track shoes contacting the ground along 157.5 inches. *Don F. Pratt Museum*

Maintenance personnel use an M543 5-ton medium wrecker to pull a power pack (the engine-transmission assembly) in Vietnam. The vehicle being serviced is an M728 combat engineer vehicle, on the basis of the M60 chassis, but the power pack and rear hull configuration duplicate those of the M48A3. *Chris Harlow*

The loader's position of this M48A3 has been fitted with an M60 machine gun, mounted with an M113 cupola bracket. Crews in Vietnam rarely operated "buttoned up"—the heat inside the vehicles being almost unbearable. Thus, with more eyes outside, it was only natural that more weapons would be fitted. *TACOM LCMC History Office*

Tanks from C Company, 1st Marine Tank Battalion, leave Con Thiên with elements of Lima Company, 3rd Battalion, 4th Marines, on a corridor patrol on January 20, 1969. The three visible tank crew members wear CVC helmets, while the tank riders sport caps or M1 helmets.

In this view of the 3rd Platoon, C Company, 1st Marine Tank Battalion, tank **also seen at left**, the missing left front fender panel is more readily apparent, as is the 5-gallon fuel can leaning against the left headlamp cluster.

The tank commander, Cpl. Robert G. Olsen, and loader, Cpl. Charles S. Yesmen, both from the 3rd Platoon, C Company, 1st Marine Tank Battalion, hang on tight as their tank climbs out of a big ditch it had to cross during Operation Pipestone Canyon, 8 miles south of Da Nang, on June 2, 1969. *Patton Museum*

Two tanks from C Company, 1st Tank Battalion, 3rd Platoon, stop and look over the terrain situation before moving on during Operation Pipestone Canyon, 8 miles south of Da Nang, on June 2, 1969. The operation was another attempt to retake the Go Noi Island area, and it involved four USMC units as well as the ROK 2nd Marine Brigade. The massive sweep was conducted for months—from May 26 through November 7. This photo was likely taken just prior to C Company's assault on enemy bunkers on the afternoon of June 2.

This M48A3 Mod B of H Company, 11th Armored Cavalry Regiment, was disabled when it ran over an antitank mine on December 27, 1969, just outside Camp Eunice. The damage to the first road wheel is evident, and the track has naturally been thrown.

Soldiers have to eat—and seemingly rarely trust others to feed them. On top of the turret of the tank in the background can be seen one of the coveted Mermite cans—insulated containers capable of keeping food (or beverages) hot or cold. On the engine deck of the disabled tank in the foreground appear to be two cases of rations. Everything has been coated with the red dust of Vietnam.

Parts of damaged track links were scattered around the area by the mine explosion, which also damaged wheels. The explosive device was estimated to be a 23-pound antitank mine.

In addition to mine damage, the fenders have received a battering from normal use. There is extensive additional stowage on the engine deck and turret. The unit markings have been applied freehand, rather than with stencils.

Beyond bending the road wheel, the blast knocked off the hub cap, revealing the bearings and spindle on which the wheel turns. Members of the 984th Land Clearing Co., 11th Cavalry, look for additional damage prior to towing the tank away.

During a break on June 23, 1969, a crewman rests atop his M48A3 of Company B, 1st Battalion, 77th Armor Regiment (Steel Tigers), during Operation Utah Mesa in the Khe Sanh area. This was the tank battalion with 1st Brigade, 5th Infantry Division (Mechanized).

With the name "Disaster" inscribed on the gun tube, this late-model M48A3 from 2nd Platoon, C Company, 1st Marine Tank Battalion, USMC, prepares to move out 15 miles southeast of Da Nang on February 12, 1970. The commander's machine gun is mounted outside the cupola, despite a Marine Corps directive forbidding this. *Patton Museum*

The predominant piece of NVA armor was the Soviet PT-76 amphibious tank. This example of such a vehicle was destroyed during the only NVA vs. US tank battle of the war, the Vietcong assault on Ben Het Special Forces camp on March 4, 1970. Engaged against M48A3s from 1st Platoon, B Company, 1st Battalion, 69th Armor Regiment, this action cost the NVA two PT-76s and a BTR-50PK amphibious armored personnel carrier. One M48A3 took a hit from a 76 mm round, which killed two crewmen. In an earlier action an M48A3 knocked out another PT-76 before the NVA crew could locate the threat.

A Marine M48A3 from Company C, 1st Marine Tank Battalion, pushes through the elephant grass near Da Nang while acting as the forward elements for Company F, 2nd Battalion, 5th Marines, on May 13, 1970. Marine infantry hitch a ride on the tank, avoiding wading through the grass themselves.

Two tanks of Company C, 1st Tank Battalion, work with Company H, 2nd Battalion, 5th Marines, while they are sweeping north of Combat Base An Hoa, 20 miles southwest of Da Nang, on May 20, 1970. The leading edges of the fenders of both tanks are somewhat battered, a common problem with the Pattons operating in country.

Crews became adept at performing routine maintenance and minor repairs themselves while operating in the field. Here, members of the 25th Infantry Division repair a compensating and idler wheel in July 1970.

These 25th Infantry Division Maintenance personnel cut away damaged portions of the fender of this M48A3 in Vietnam in August 1970. Despite efforts to strengthen the fenders, they remained susceptible to damage from heavy vegetation. Presumably the small-arms ammunition boxes sitting just inches away no longer contain munitions.

Many structures in Cambodia would succumb as easily to the mass of the M48A3 as did the vegetation of the nation. Here, units of E Troop, 11th Armored Cavalry, push through the outskirts of Snuol, Cambodia, on May 4, 1970.

An OH-6A light observation helicopter passes overhead as members of E Troop, 11th Armored Cavalry ride M48A3 tanks past damaged buildings on the outskirts of Snuol, Cambodia, on May 4, 1970.

An M48A3 and its crew join M113A1 crews of the 2nd Battalion, 47th Infantry Regiment (Mechanized), 9th Infantry Division, setting up an overnight site during operations in the Chalang and Srok (District) Memot, Cambodia, in the first half of May 1970.

Members of H Troop, 11th Armored Cavalry, aboard an M48A3 tank, take a break during combat operations north of Snuol, Cambodia, on May 6, 1970. The tarp over the stowage rack protected items not only from rain, but also from snakes and insects dropping in from brush and taking residence in the gear.

Bridges were key points in Vietnam, and tanks were often employed to defend these critical supply routes. Such is the case with this M48A3 defending a bridge on the road to Pleiku.

This tank has been knocked out and the final road-wheel station blown completely off. There has also been damage to the fenders and engine deck. *TACOM LCMC History Office*

Two M48A3s sit next to an M42 Duster in the Class 7 storage area of the 625th Supply and Service Company on Wunder Beach in June 1970. During the Vietnam War, the Pattons were cycled back to the Track Vehicle Reclamation Center in Sagami, Japan, for overhaul.

This M48A3 of the 3rd Squadron, 11th Armored Cavalry Regiment, operating from Fire Support Base Bandit II in November 1970, reminds us that the combat vehicle has not been built whose crew felt it had enough room for stowage, had enough armor, or carried enough ammo. Ammo cans, track links, and ration cases cover virtually every inch of the tank.

M48A3 tanks from M Troop, 3rd Squadron, 11th Armored Cavalry Regiment, move across an open field during a reconnaissance-in-force mission north of Fire Support Base Bandit II. This tank carries numerous ammunition boxes on its fenders, and ration cases on its turret, during the late November 1970 operation.

GIs warily eye the surrounding brush as two M48A3s maneuver through the jungle of Vietnam. A canvas cover over the xenon searchlight prevents glare to minimize detection, and a case of grenades is at the feet of one of the lookouts. This M48A3 tank from M Troop, 3rd Squadron, 11th Armored Cavalry Regiment, was photographed during a reconnaissance-in-force mission north of Fire Support Base Bandit II in late November 1970.

The G305 turret riser can be plainly seen here. This riser provided the commander a 360-degree range of vision from inside the vehicle. In Vietnam, most TCs (tank commanders) fought outside the turret, negating the benefit of this riser. The machine gun on this tank has been relocated to a position on top of the cupola to facilitate this type of fighting.

The commander's machine gun on this tank has also been relocated, although using a different style of mounting than the one shown at left. Extra boxes of ammo, already open, are kept at the ready on the turret roof.

Empty cartridge cases litter the ground as tanks of the 11th Armored Cavalry Regiment test-fire their guns on the firing range before moving to the stand-down area on January 23, 1971. All three of these tanks are covered with the red dust of Vietnam, and considerable additional stowage.

An M48A3 from the 197th Infantry Brigade fires during a demonstration of night defense perimeter techniques employed in Vietnam during a training exercise at Fort Benning, Georgia, in June 1971. The M48A3 offered the most protection of any US armor fielded in Vietnam, and its firepower was often critical to defending forward bases.

Rocket-propelled grenades (RPGs) were a constant threat—and capable of inflicting crew casualties. Many tankers fitted their vehicles with various improvised devices aimed at protecting themselves from RPG attack. The turret of this M48A3 of 3rd Squadron, 4th Cavalry, is completely covered in sandbags for just this reason. *Patton Museum*

The Patton remained in Vietnam after the US departed. These M48A3s were operated by the Army of the Republic of Vietnam (ARVN) and are seen here in position along National Highway 9 in April 1972. *Patton Museum*

The ARVN was supplied large numbers of the M48A3, which typically were in the standard as-issued configuration like this one with the cupola-mounted machine gun, rather than the externally mounted weapon favored by Americans. *Patton Museum*

The ARVN tankers proved themselves most proficient in the use of the M48A3 but were plagued by a shortage of spare parts—and equally importantly, by an overwhelming numerical disadvantage to Communist armor after the 1973 ceasefire. *Patton Museum*

In some instances, the lack of spares reduced the Pattons to use as pillboxes. The April 1972 introduction of the 9M14M Malyutka wire-guided antitank missile brought a new threat to the Patton, and several were lost to these Soviet-made missiles in the succeeding months. *Patton Museum*

This ARVN 20th Tank Regiment M48A3 was photographed in April 1972 while in a defensive position on the Đông Hà Line. ARVN use of the Patton was hampered by the lack of adequate quantities of support equipment, such as the M88 retriever.

This restored example of the M48A3 Mod B, one of three in the US, was previously displayed at the Patton Museum at Ft. Knox, Kentucky. This tank was presented to the United States by Vietnam in the 1990s. It is marked as B11, 1-69 Armor, the mount of Spec 4 Dwight H. Johnson, who was awarded the Medal of Honor protecting his tank and wounded crew members in January 1968. M48A3s were converted from earlier M48A1 models to update the tanks and ease the logistics load of providing spare parts for both the M48 and M60 series. Detail differences in production runs of tanks from Ford, GM, and Chrysler required different conversion kits. *Scott Taylor*

The two front road-wheel stations were equipped with friction snubbers, which replaced the shock absorbers of earlier models. The large brackets on the hull side mount spring bumpers for the swing arms that limit their upward travel. The M48A3 received new double spring bumpers at the first road-wheel station. The link between the first swing arm and the compensating idler wheel mount provides slack in the track if the first road wheel travels downward. The road wheels and idlers were composed of steel wheels with a rubber tire pressed on. The dimensions of the rubber tire are 26 by 6 inches. The wheel was bolted to a central hub assembly carrying a wheel bearing. The central cap carried a grease fitting for quick lubrication of the bearing. Note the shape of the center guide teeth on the T97 track.

The suspension swing arms were fixed to the end of the torsion bars that were anchored to the opposite side of the hull floor. The first swing arm, a new heavier design on the M48A3, was attached to the compensating idler to maintain proper track tension over rough terrain, to reduce the likelihood of a thrown track. This style of idler was common with the M60 and was new to the M48A3 conversion. The rubber tires were molded in a clamshell mold, causing a parting seam down the center of the tire. The tires made contact with the rubber portion of the inside of the 28-inch-wide track. The large mount for the spring bumper on the first road wheel is used to dampen the blow of any large bump for the first road-wheel station.

The link between the idler mount and first swing arm is hexagonal and rotates to adjust track tension. Viewed from the front, the link's forward section is threaded to allow adjustment of the length of the link, thus setting the track tension. This system for adjusting track tension is common throughout the Pershing and Patton series.

The contours of the ballistic elliptical-shaped hull make necessary a housing to carry the end of each torsion bar. These castings carry a bearing for the free end of the torsion bar and anchor the torsion bar that crosses the hull floor from the opposite-side suspension. Typical of all American cast parts, the piece is adorned with an identifying part number.

The T97 track has vulcanized rubber pads cast around a metal skeleton. These pads make contact with the ground and provide a smooth surface on the inner face for contacting the road wheel's rubber tire. Note the worn surface of the center guide tooth, made bright by contact with the road wheels and return rollers.

Friction snubbers serve the same purpose as a shock absorber, but rather than being filled with oil, the inner and outer tubes contact each other, lined with material similar to brake linings, resisting movement by friction. They have greater service life in heavy applications. The mounting brackets for the friction snubbers are cast steel. They are marked with various casting numbers and foundry marks.

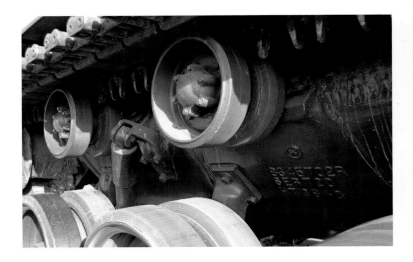

The vertical weld seam on the hull side denotes that this lower hull is of the built-up variety rather than a single-piece casting. The casting marks on the hull side denote the manufacturer, Continental Foundry and Machine Co., the part number, series production, and a heat treatment code. The foundry marks are just below the fourth return roller on the right hull side, even with the spring bumper mount.

The track support return rollers were also rubber-tired like the road wheels. They were constructed of two pressed-steel wheels paired and bolted to a center hub. The hubs and bearings could be serviced or replaced separately from the wheel. The center cap was equipped with a grease fitting for lubrication purposes.

The track-tensioning roller characteristic of the M48A1 was removed from the rear suspension during the M48A3 conversion. The large air cleaner boxes of the new AVDS-1790 diesel power pack are mounted on top of each fender outboard of the engine deck. Spare track links are attached to the turret sides of this vehicle.

The last road-wheel station of the right suspension is equipped with a friction snubber. Note the axle housing present behind the road wheel for the absent track tensioner's swing arm.

The drive sprockets on the M48 series are mounted at the rear. They are two forged, eleven-toothed sprockets mounted to a central hub. The barrel of the outer hub has openings that both lighten its weight and allow mud that builds up in the center a path to exit. The rings at the center of the hub form a trench for the guide teeth of the track and help prevent thrown tracks.

The massive rear exhaust grilles were added in the conversion from M48A1 to M48A3. Exhaust gases were routed under the engine deck cover and diffused through the rear grilles to reduce the infrared signature of the vehicle, especially when viewed from the front. The engine doors were built from large steel strips and angled to deflect small-arms fire and were constructed of heavy-enough material to prevent small-arms fire from entering the engine compartment. The panel surrounded by bolts in the top of the right-hand door is removable for installing the deepwater-fording snorkel for the engine. *John Charvat*

Many identifying features of the M48A3 are seen from the left rear corner. On the fender top is the left-side air cleaner box for the new diesel engine. The M1 cupola now sits on a spacer ring atop the turret, an identifying feature of the M48A3 Mod B. A stowage bracket for the searchlight has been added to the turret blower cover. The rear fender extensions have the embossed X-shaped reinforcement. *John Charvat*

The fender is damaged near the left-side air filter box. The air filter elements were loaded into the boxes through doors in their side. This type of fender damage made servicing the filter difficult, if not impossible, without repair. Later-style filter boxes on the M48A5 and M60 series were designed to be serviced from the top for this reason.

The trail of the flow of mud down the hull side gives a good impression of the complex contours of the lower hull casting forward of the final-drive assemblies. The hull narrowed at this point and flattened to allow the attachment of the final-drive components. *Chun Hsu*

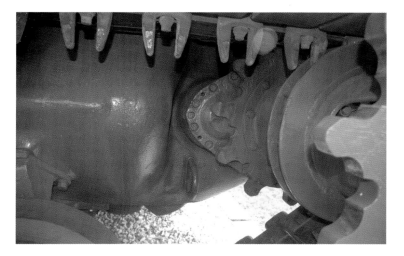

The bolts that attach the drive sprocket plates to the hubs are secured on the backside with nuts. These drive sprockets are common to both the M48 and M60 series of main battle tanks.

One of the torsion bar support castings on the left side of the lower hull. Most American foundries used a simplified logo on their parts to denote the producer, important for warranty consideration. Here the complete name "Ford" is used on the part.

The turret of this M48A3 is reversed and the main gun is placed in the travel lock. The turret is covered with links of spare track. Extra track links were commonly used by M48 crews in Vietnam as standoff protection against shaped-charge antitank weapons. *Chun Hsu*

The linkages of the compensating idler wheel, swing arms, and friction snubbers worked in concert to absorb bumps as the vehicle moved forward. Capable of a 30 mph top speed, the tank could hit bumps with a great deal of force. The idler link worked to keep the track properly tensioned over bumps and uneven terrain.

The M48A3 with full combat load weighed in at over 50 tons. This meant that all suspension components had to be robust to take the punishment of use over rough terrain. The contours of the lower hull casting are visible behind the suspension components.

The road-wheel tires were extremely tough, solid vulcanized rubber. But even the hardest rubber can be chipped or damaged, as we see on this front left wheel. The link to the compensating idler is directly behind the wheel.

The upper hull side mount for the left front road-wheel station snubber. The mounting position was machined and tapped onto the rough casting of the lower hull to accept the bolts and flat surfaces of all the suspension components. The surface of the area around the mount has been machined to facilitate mounting. *Chun Hsu*

With the drive sprockets at the rear, the front idler wheel set the track tension. This wheel was identical and interchangeable with the road wheels, which helped simplify parts supply. The M48 series was equipped with live tracks that were kept quite tight without any sag. The suspension of the M48 series made the vehicle sit quite high and provided ground clearance of over 16 inches below the hull. This resulted in the tank having a very high silhouette in comparison to its Soviet-built adversaries. *Chun Hsu*

The outer edge of the lower hull front was contoured to accept the mount for the compensating idler wheel. This gave the hull a very boatlike appearance as it transitioned forward from its elliptical cross section. *Chun Hsu*

The M48A3 conversions received new fenders, braces, and headlight stations. The headlights were the new composite removable types common with the M60 series. Here the lights are removed, giving a good view of the heavy guards. The hull front has received an antislip coating to make entry into the driver's position safer.

Here the headlight is in place. The units carried a standard clear sealed beam lamp and a blackout driving light on each side. The massive thickness of the guards is seen from straight ahead. Note the details of the embossed "X" reinforcement in the fender front panel. *John Charvat*

The front fenders of the M48A3 included a flap-type fitting that projected below the midline of the hull. This aided in keeping mud and dust from being thrown up into the driver's field of view or onto his periscopes. The boxlike fitting ahead of the headlight is a portion of the old M48A1 fender brace. *John Charvat*

The left-side headlight was also updated in the M48A3 program. The composite headlight assemblies could be unplugged and removed. The opening was then plugged to keep moisture from the inside. The earlier models had a three-lamp system behind a much-lighter guard, which was often damaged in service. The fitting with the red handles is the firing mechanism for the internal fire-extinguisher system. This could be set off by the exiting driver or by brave ground troops in an emergency. *John Charvat*

The new fenders on the M48A3 were much heavier in construction, with more bracing than previous models. There are several patterns seen on various vehicles that were necessary for converting tanks with detail differences from different manufacturers. *John Charvat*

The M48A3 fender design incorporated large "X" embossed reinforcements that added strength without adding weight to the upper panels as well as the front. Even with the heavier construction, these fenders are often seen damaged, modified, or removed while in service in Vietnam. *Chun Hsu*

A mannequin is in the driver's position with the seat raised. The driver's hatch would open with the three hull-mounted periscopes in place, but it was necessary to remove the periscope from the hatch itself. Also visible are the details of the left side of the front hull, including the headlight suite, the external control for the fire extinguisher system, a lift ring, and the plate blanking off the old position for the crew heater exhaust. *John Charvat*

The driver's hatch is a rather tight fit for operating with the head out. This hatch is significantly larger than the original hatch design on the T48 tanks. *Don Moriarty*

The rear edge of the hatch plate was beveled. All the external components of the hatch, including the periscope cover, are steel castings. The parts numbers are visible on both the cover and periscope mount. A circular weld seam is visible where the hatch pivot is attached to the hatch. The hatch lowered to rest on the post at lower left, which was also notched to act as a stop. *John Charvat*

The driver's hatch is extremely close to the lower edge of the gun shield. The driver's hatch rested on two rodlike projections when opened. This kept the pivot hinge from carrying the weight of the heavy hatch. The forward rod, *lower left*, was notched to hold the hatch in place while the vehicle was in motion. Operating the vehicle with the hatch open and the seat raised was normally reserved for road use, with the turret traversed to the rear and the main gun in the travel lock. The three fixed periscopes in the hull were model M27; simple prisms of armored glass with a sheet-metal casing that could be quickly removed and replaced if damaged. The external portion includes a hinged cover that is spring loaded to close when the periscope is removed. The periscope is surrounded by a rubber seal to keep moisture from leaking in around the sides.

Right: With the turret reversed to the travel position, the indentation in the lower bustle casting is visible. This allowed the driver more space to operate with his head out of the hatch. Part of the M48A3 conversion was replacement of the crew compartment heater with that of the M60 series. The location of the new heater, to the driver's right, required a new routing of the exhaust for the heater out of the hull and over the right-side fender ahead of the fender stowage box, to which the exhaust pipe brackets of the crew compartment heater are affixed to the fender brace. The addition of the air cleaners for the diesel engine conversion made the relocation of the vehicle's tow cables necessary. They were installed below the turret bustle rack in the clips next to the bracket for the 5-gallon liquid container. *Chun Hsu*

Below: The general layout of the M48A3 is shown in this right-side view. The turret is rotated to the travel position and is covered by spare track links; a spare road wheel hangs from the AN/VSS-1 searchlight storage rack. There are two spare road wheels mounted on the searchlight storage mount, and a spare return roller wheel on the bustle rack. *Chun Hsu*

The fenders are fitted with stowage boxes on either side of the turret. The boxes are bolted in place to brackets on the fenders and braces fore and aft. Just to the rear of the box is the front of the side-loading air cleaner box. *Chun Hsu*

The new diesel engine for the M48A3 was equipped with larger external air cleaners. These were housed on boxes on both fenders. The elements were serviced through doors on the sides of the boxes, the door hinges being at the rear.

The front inboard corners of the air cleaner boxes were angled for turret clearance. The angled pipes on the front of the box are the air intakes. The fitting on the inboard side of the box connects the filter to the engine. The brackets on the air cleaner are for mounting a hand-operated fuel pump to pump diesel fuel from 55-gallon drums or other vehicles into the tank. *John Charvat*

The forward cooling-intake grille door incorporates the fittings for the air cleaner boxes. The airflow in this area is directed through large engine-oil coolers on each side of the engine, as well as across the individual air-cooled cylinders of the engine. *Chun Hsu*

The details of the right-rear corner of the vehicle include the rear engine air intake grille, the right half of the infrared-suppressing engine deck cover, and an additional stowage box aft of the air cleaner box. *Chun Hsu*

Looking forward along the upper edge of the right hull, the contour curves around the rear-side engine intake grille doors. Note the shape of the rear fender stowage box, slanted to match the shape of the hull side. *Chun Hsu*

The shape of the lower hull casting is quite complex in the area around the transmission and final drives. The square covers at the top are for access doors to the transmission. The round plates bolted into the hull casting are for access to the brake rods.

The sheet-metal fender skirt curves down around the final-drive housing and is attached to the bottom of the taillight housing. These housings, part of the M48A3 Mod B package, were a new addition during the conversion and are far more robust than the older mounts. The filler plug for the final drive is in the center of the photograph.

The fender skirt does not exactly match the contours of the final-drive housing. Details of the exhaust door grilles are visible behind the right-rear fender. The new mountings for the taillights are quite massive on the M48A3 Mod B. Most of the modifications made to the tanks were designed to address issues that the troops were having with the M48 series in the field. No doubt the thick vegetation of the Vietnam jungles had some effect in this improvement. *Chun Hsu*

The new diesel engine was a development of the Continental AV-1790 gasoline engine series of the earlier tanks. This made the engine relatively easy to adapt to the gasoline-fueled M48A1. This also made the infrared-suppression engine deck and rear exhaust grilles very similar to those of the M48A2. Handles were mounted on the bottom edge of the exhaust grilles, which would be the coolest place to touch. These doors opened to expose the transmission compartment. The vehicle was equipped with a towing pintle attached at the center rear of the lower hull to a heavy steel bracket. Behind the tow pintle is the central transmission access. *Chun Hsu*

The infrared-suppression engine deck installation required the movement of the gun travel lock to its rear edge. The travel lock contacts the tube just behind the fume extractor. The engine deck had a layer of insulation to maximize the amount of heat that exited through the rear grilles. *Chun Hsu*

The inner side of the left-side stowage box is angled for clearance. The inner front corner of the air cleaner boxes is also angled. The fender brackets are very heavy assemblies with large lightening holes that bolt to large brackets welded to the hull side. *Chun Hsu*

The left-side fender stowage box, seen with the turret, traversed to the rear. The spare track links are connected to the turret-side grab rail by the center guide horns. *Chun Hsu*

All the handles on the engine deck doors and air cleaner boxes lie flush with the surface. The handles are designed so as not to encumber a crewman walking on the deck to service the vehicle. *Chun Hsu*

The left-side forward engine air intake grille is made up of four separate cast parts, all hinged to fold outward. With the deck removed and the grilles and rear doors opened, access to the power pack was completely unobstructed. *Chun Hsu*

The air intake tubes are mounted on the forward portion of the left-side air cleaner box. In the lower left is visible the left-side fuel filler cover. The hinges of the cover have been removed on this example. *Chun Hsu*

The engine deck was constructed of a number of formed steel pieces welded together to form the long sloping shape. The front portion of the deck has openings for three rectangular engine-access hatches.

The new fender sections were added during the M48A3 conversion. Installation of the rear exhaust grille doors made it necessary to relocate the rear hull lifting rings. The antiskid texture on all the upper surfaces was not applied at the time of conversion and is a later addition to this example.

The gun barrel is locked in the rear position in its folding travel lock. Travel locks were used to save wear and tear on fire control system components and the gun stabilizer. The lock clamped to the barrel just aft of the fume extractor. *Chun Hsu*

The travel lock was a rather simple affair made up of steel castings and a hinge assembly. The upper clamp was held in place by the large single wing-handled bolt. The rod arrangement at the bottom of the lock is a stand to hold it upright while the barrel is put in place.

The forward engine-access hatches are secured with bolts and are lifted out with the flush folding handles at the edges. The access panels are made as three separate parts to make their weight manageable for lifting by hand. *Chun Hsu*

The slope of the hull-side casting is evident in this view. The intake grille doors were cast to fit the complex curves and to close on the edge of each consecutive door for support. The bolt in the bracket on the edge of the hull plate could be used to prevent all the doors on one side from being opened. *Chun Hsu*

With the turret traversed to the front, it is evident that the forward sloped portion of the deck was necessary for proper clearance of the turret bustle. The clips along the bottom edge of the turret rear are used to stow the tow cable, missing from this example.

The upper hull casting curved upward to meet the turret in the area behind the driver's position. The turret ring diameter on the M48 and M60 series tanks was 85 inches. The clips on the turret side beside the track blocks are for storing tow cables.

This is a very complete example of an M48A3 on display at Ft. Riley, Kansas. It is missing only a few fittings, including the fabric covers for the gun shield and cupola. The gun shield on the M48 series was homogeneous steel armor casting 4½ inches thick. The circular plate surrounding the barrel is a removable plate, allowing quick access to change the gun tube. The lift rings are welded to the shield. This tank is equipped with the less common Y-shaped blast deflector on the 90 mm main gun.

The canvas dustcover for the gun shield is made up of pieces of canvas cloth impregnated with a weatherproofing plastic material. Various pieces were stitched together to match the contours of the shield over protrusions such as the lift rings. All necessary openings were reinforced around their edges. A bellows-like attachment sealed around the gun tube and allowed for recoil movement when firing the gun. The metallic ball-like fittings are for mounting the searchlight and are similar in design to ball trailer hitches.

The cover was held in place and sealed to the turret face by bolted clamps. This decaying cover shows the internal structure of the wire supports that stiffened the area of the cover between the shield and the face of the turret. The nuts holding the ball mounts for the searchlight are at the top center of the picture. The openings for the direct-sight telescope and the coaxially mounted machine gun are covered in tape.

The AN/VSS-1 xenon searchlight is installed on this example. The power supply for the searchlight exited the turret through the left front roof and connected to the back of the device. The power supply cord is not attached to the light in this view. The rear housing of the light has screened openings for cooling air.

The xenon searchlight was developed for the M60 series and was first introduced to the M48 with the M48A3 and M48A1E2 conversions of 1967. The 2.2-kilowatt searchlight had both visible light and infrared capability and provided the tanks with night-fighting capability. The light is covered in this view.

The searchlight was equipped with a handle on each side to aid in moving and positioning the heavy assembly for mounting on the gun shield. The clamps on the top and bottom of the housing allowed the front of the housing to be removed for servicing the element or replacing the lens. *John Charvat*

The searchlight's canvas cover was held in place by two web straps that looped over a rail on the rear of the housing. The position of the lamp could be aligned relative to the gun tube by the adjusting nuts on the top mount. *John Charvat*

The power supply cord for the light is properly positioned in this view. The cord was protected by a thick black rubber cover over the internal leads. The end was equipped with multiple-end connectors that plugged into the rear of the lamp. The forward turret lift ring is visible at the center right. *Don Moriarty*

The rear bracket attached the searchlight to the gun shield, locking on the ball fittings seen earlier. Each of the three mounting points was like the hitch on a trailer tongue, with a T-handle that locked it in place. The adjusting nuts are visible at the top center of the mount. *John Charvat*

The M41 90 mm gun was a development of the weapon first used on the M26 Pershing and M36 tank destroyer late in World War II. During the years following the war, ammunition for the weapon improved radically, greatly increasing its penetrating power. *Don Moriarty*

The T-shaped blast deflector was the most common type on the M48 series. The fitting was designed to route the blast of the weapon out the sides of the muzzle rather than downward, which would stir up debris and obscure the gunner's view for subsequent shots. *Chun Hsu*

The Y-shaped blast deflector was an earlier item and less common on M48s. It replaced a tubular deflector and single-baffle muzzle brake used on the M47. The rifling is visible on the interior of the gun tube through the bore opening in the blast deflector. *John Charvat*

The bore evacuator was made of relatively light sheet steel and covered small perforations in the gun tube wall. The cover kept moisture from entering the gun tube and spoiling the bore. Note the casting seam along the side of the blast deflector.

The armored cover for the M32 periscope was bolted to the turret roof with Allen-head screws at the rear. The M32 replaced the earlier M20 unit on the M48A2 and A3. This was the main sight for the gunner and was linked to the fire control system. *Chun Hsu*

The periscope was equipped with an armored cover that could be pivoted from the turret interior to protect the periscope when not in use. The direct-sight periscope mounted in the gun shield served as a backup in case of damage to the periscope. The rotated L-shaped guard was to prevent a machine gun mounted on the cupola from being fired into the AN/VSS-1 searchlight. The odd shape of the guard for the xenon searchlight is necessary to avoid obstructing the field of view of the gunner's periscope. *Chun Hsu*

The armored cover in its open position reveals the armored glass face of the M32 periscope. The commander's cupola received several modifications during the M48A3 conversion. The most noticeable is the spacer ring, including nine armored glass blocks, added as part of the M48A3 Mod B package. The ring was an attempt to solve the problem of cramped space and limited visibility that had plagued the M1 cupola since its introduction. The new vision block ring greatly increased visibility within the cupola. It did not solve the problem of limited ammunition space for the .50-caliber machine gun or ease the task of reloading the weapon. Many crews continued the practice of mounting the gun atop the cupola in service in Vietnam. *Don Moriarty*

Another modification to the cupola was the addition of a fairing to the spent-ammunition chute on the right side. The earlier arrangement had at times jammed up with disintegrating links and spent cases when firing the machine gun. Note the texture and foundry marks on the cast components of the cupola. The new fairing also kept the links and cases from fouling the area between the ring and the cupola. The square projection welded to the cupola shield is a mount for relocating the machine gun to the exterior. *Chun Hsu*

Yet another modification to the cupola that was carried out due to feedback from crews in Vietnam is the bulged hatch cover. This replaced the earlier design, giving the commander more headroom in the cupola and more-comfortable access to his sight in the cupola roof. An M28 periscope that incorporated the sight for the machine gun was installed in a cupola roof mount with an armored guard. *Chun Hsu*

A raised ledge was incorporated into the upper edge of the vision ring casting to protect the joint between the ring and the cupola. To avoid rainwater pooling inside the ledge, there are three breaks that serve as drains. The casting marks on the cupola body are ahead of the M28 periscope mount. The M28 periscope mount was fixed in the roof and rotated with the cupola, aligned in azimuth with the machine gun. The sight was monocular, with a covered eyepiece in the interior. The external guard was as much for protecting the sight from the crew as from damage due to enemy fire. *Chun Hsu*

A view of the cupola from the ground gives an idea of the extreme height of the vehicle. With the new vision block ring, the overall height was increased to over 10½ feet. Note the contours of the turret casting around the right-side rangefinder bulge. *John Charvat*

The additional height of the bulged cupola hatch cover is evident when viewed from the rear. The new cover eliminated the two vision blocks of the older design. The turret rear of the M48A3 mounts a large ventilator blower under a domed armored cover. Fittings for antenna mounts are on either side of the turret. The bracket in the center is the latch to hold the open loader's escape hatch, which on this example is missing its catch.

The semicircular hatch for the loader is similar to US designs dating back to the M4 Sherman, which sits flush with the turret roof when closed. The large springs assist the crewman in opening the heavy hatch. The trench in the roof armor to the edge of the turret is a drain for rainwater that might pool around the hatch opening.

The fixture for storing the searchlight is seen at the left, attached to the bulge in the turret bustle, which houses the ventilator. The turret stowage rack wrapped around the entire turret rear, slightly farther forward on the right side. These racks are seen in combat crammed with a wide variety of the crew's personal gear. The screen insert in the rack is not a part of the original M48A3 conversion, being added during a later update, as were the two horizontal bars on the rack, which could support spare road wheels.

This example has had the searchlight storage rack modified to carry a spare road wheel. This was not uncommon in Vietnam, where mine damage to road wheels was a constant problem. The rear turret rack carries a spare return roller wheel, and an additional 5-gallon-can rack.

The bulge on each side of the turret houses the end of the mechanical range-finding device. The commander focused two images from the optics in each end of the device that drove a mechanical link to the fire control computer, to quickly establish the range to the target. The front of the cover has an opening for the sights of the rangefinder. The turret casting is very subtly shaped to match the contours of the various turret fittings, such as the rangefinder, gunner's periscope cover, and cupola ring on the right side.

The left side of the turret casting is not as steep as the right. The loader sits farther back in the turret on the left than the gunner's position on the right. The left-side cover for the rangefinder is at the top center of the photograph.

The aperture for the left-side rangefinder cover is machined into a prominent bulge in the turret casting. This brings the mating surfaces to a vertical finish, allowing the cover to rotate in elevation along with the gun barrel. The fire control system of the M48 series constantly evolved and was updated throughout its service life. The first T48s reached production without the M17 coincidence rangefinder but were equipped with the covers to accept later upgrades. The details of the trunnion for the cupola machine gun mount are visible behind the rangefinder cover. *John Charvat*

The left-side rangefinder cover is seen from above, along with the bulge of the turret wall. The opening in the cover is sealed with tape. Spare links of T97 track are fastened to the grab rail below. The antiskid texture on the turret roof is a later addition. *Chun Hsu*

CHAPTER 6
M48A4

A surplus of turrets for the "Tank, 105 mm Gun, M60" in the mid-1960s was the impetus for the development of the M48A4. It initially was designated the XM735 tank and then the M48A1E3 before being designated the M48A4. Two examples were built, which were based on M48A1 chassis refitted to M48A3 standards. One of them is shown here in this photo from September 11, 1967. Development of the M48A4 did not proceed past these two examples. *TACOM LCMC History Office*

In the mid-1960s, the Army was enthralled with antitank missiles, especially the Shillelagh. Serious consideration was given to refit much of the M60 fleet with missile-firing turrets, akin to the M60A2. This program would result in large numbers of surplus M60 turrets armed with 105 mm guns. In December 1965, a program was initiated to install such a turret on an M48A3 chassis. Initially known as the XM735, two tanks were so modified. Because the turret basket of the M60 was deeper than that of the M48, spacer rings had to be utilized to adapt the M48 hull to the new turret. The outer ring provided ballistic protection, while the inner ring provided the mechanical interface and lifted the turret.

Inside the hull, the ammunition stowage was revised to accommodate the 105 mm ammunition. This was done by using M60A1 ammo racks adapted to the elliptical shape of the M48 hull. Following successful testing at Fort Knox, the new configuration was designated M48A4 and program-approved to convert 243 M48A1s to M48A4 standard. However, the M60A2 program was greatly reduced; thus there were few surplus M60 gun turrets available, and accordingly the M48A4 program was canceled.

The M60 turret on the M48A4 tank had an M19 cupola of noticeably different design than the M1 cupola of the M48s. The M68 105 mm gun had a bore evacuator toward the center of the barrel and lacked a muzzle brake. Adapter rings were necessary on the hull to raise the turret in order to make the turret basket fit in the opening. This M48A4 and the one in the preceding photo was USA number 9A9849. *TACOM LCMC History Office*

CHAPTER 7

M48A5

The American withdrawal from Vietnam was not the end of the M48's service life with the US Army, and the cancellation of the M48A4 was not the final effort to create a 105 mm armed M48. Rather, the venerable M48 was upgraded yet again to include many of the improvements that the Israelis had introduced during their extensive, and successful, use of M48-series tanks in combat.

Anniston Army Depot was contracted to upgrade 501 M48A3 tanks, five of which were test vehicles, to M48A5 configuration, which was to be the final incarnation of the M48 in US service. The first two test articles were delivered in June 1975, and the final three the next month. Series delivery began in October of the same year and was completed in December 1976.

Chief of the improvements incorporated in the M48A5 was the mounting of an M68 105 mm gun (British L7)—the same weapon that was used in the M60. Not insignificant was the installation of T142 track, a new turret basket, and ammunition stowage for the 105 mm ammunition.

Initially the tanks retained the M1 cupola and G305 spacer ring, but in August 1976, after serial numbers A3001 through A3999 had been produced, the turret and spacer ring were replaced on the Anniston line with a low-profile, Israeli-produced Urdan cupola. The hatch on this cupola could be moved to a partially open position, which provided the commander with considerable protection but allowed him to peer out. The two-position scissors mount for the M60D machine gun included on the cupola allowed the gun to be fired from either the raised or collapsed position. Tanks equipped with the Urdan cupola were designated M48A5PI (product improvement), but after the low-profile cupola was retrofitted to the M48A5 fleet, the PI designation was dropped.

On the basis of the success of this program, Anniston converted two M48A1s to M48A5 standard. These tanks were delivered in August 1976, and after their approval, a program got underway that would see more M48A1s converted to M48A5 configuration, until finally 2,069 M48A5s had been produced.

Most of the M48A5 production was shipped to National Guard and Reserve units, but 140 of the vehicles were shipped to active US Army battalions in Korea in June and July 1978. Ultimately, the M48 series was totally withdrawn from US service, with some of the vehicles being scrapped, others sold overseas, and still others dumped into the sea to serve as the basis for artificial reefs.

The M48A5 was a second and more successful effort to mate the 105 mm gun to the M48. Designated the XM736 and the M48A3E1 before being standardized as the M48A5, it featured an M48-type turret. This test vehicle had an M1 cupola mounted on a vision-block ring, but production vehicles would use a low-profile cupola developed by the Israeli Defense Forces (IDF). *TACOM LCMC History Office*

M48A5, USA number JA0001, is seen in this view. Ultimately, a total of 2,069 M48A5s were converted from M48A3 and, later, M48A1 chassis, spanning from 1975 to 1979. *TACOM LCMC History Office*

The designers of the M48A5 drew on recent Israeli experience with improving their M48 tanks. One visible result of this influence was the use of the IDF-type low-profile commander's cupola, as seen on this restored M48A5. Also visible were the additional pintle sockets to the front and side of the loader's hatch, permitting the installation of a machine gun. *John Charvat*

The M48A5 tank was armed with the M68 105 mm gun on a modified M87 mount. It had a 7.62 mm coaxial machine gun and a 7.62 mm machine gun on the cupola. The tracks on this vehicle are the T142, with replaceable octagonal rubber pads. *John Charvat*

The left headlight array, like the right one, contains a service headlight, infrared headlight, blackout driving light, and blackout marker lamp, in a housing with a quick-release nut below it. To the rear of the headlight array are the exterior handles and guard for the internal fire-extinguisher system. *John Charvat*

The right headlight array is identical in layout to the left one. The right brush guard, headlight array, and lifting eye are viewed from the side. The upper bows of the headlight brush guards were bolted to the lower elements and the brace, allowing for easy replacement. *John Charvat*

The fronts of the fenders of the M48A5 had X-shaped stampings for added strength. All three of the driver's periscopes are raised in this photo. On the gun shield, the dustcover has openings for the three mounting lugs for a searchlight, above the gun barrel. Pockets on the dustcover fit over the lifting lugs on the shield. *John Charvat*

The gun shield covers for the M48 tanks were fabricated from Type II Class 4 coated nylon cloth, bound on the edges with 1-inch nylon tape. Over the fender is the personnel heater exhaust pipe. On the turret is the cover for the right rangefinder: on this model, it was the M17B1C rangefinder. To the front of the cupola are the gunner's M32 periscope and its guard.

An unrestored M48A5 is viewed from the right rear with its turret traversed, providing a good view of the xenon searchlight. Inside the cast-aluminum searchlight housing with a glass lens in front is the spherical-shaped lamp housing, below which are the drive motors, and behind which is the primary reflector. *John Charvat*

The xenon searchlight is viewed from its left side. The searchlight could operate in visible-light and infrared-light modes. The searchlight was affixed to the gun shield via a shock mount fixture, and it moved in unison with the 105 mm gun's traverse and elevation.

The bore evacuator of the M68 105 mm gun of the M48A5 tank is seen from the left side. It is mounted with its front-to-rear horizontal centerline above the corresponding centerline of the main gun. The block-shaped object to the front of the headlight array is a vestigial mount for the front right outrigger that originally supported the front of the fender on M48s up through the M48A3. *John Charvat*

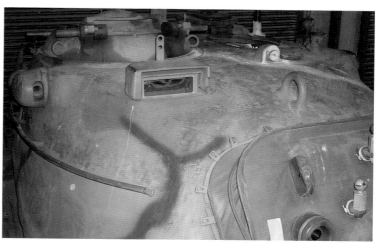

Facing toward the rear, on the turret roof to the front of the loader's hatch is the receptacle for the electrical cable for the xenon searchlight, with a screw-on cover on the receptacle. To the left is the gunner's periscope and guard, to the rear of which is the IDF-type cupola, which is traversed to the rear. *John Charvat*

Elements on the roof of an M48A5 turret are viewed from the right front. Note the lifting ring to the rear of the top of the gun shield and the small lifting rings on the cupola. In the foreground are tabs for securing the perimeter of the dustcover of the gun shield to the turret. *John Charvat*

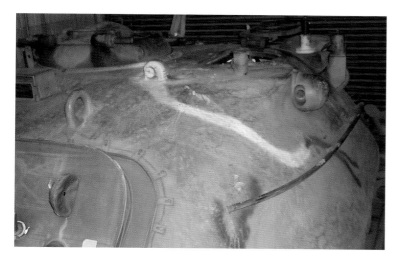

In a view from the front left of the turret to the front of the loader's hatch is a socket for an M60D 7.62 mm machine gun mount. On the top of the socket is a screw-on cap with a retainer chain. The light-colored fixture at the center of the photo is the receptacle for the xenon searchlight. *John Charvat*

Visible through the loader's hatch to the right are 105 mm ammunition storage tubes inside the turret. On the inner face of the hatch door are a cushion to protect the loader's head, a handle, and a latch for locking the door. On the left, on the cupola is the mount for the commander's M60D 7.62 mm machine gun: a scissors-type design that could be set at either a high or a low position. *John Charvat*

On the turret roof to the right side of the loader's hatch is a white-colored radio antenna mount and, to the lower right of the photo, another socket for a pintle-mounted M60D 7.62 mm machine gun, with a protective cap on it. With this socket and the one to the front of this hatch, the loader could position his machine gun to fire to the front or to the side. *John Charvat*

The radio antenna mount, the loader's side machine-gun socket, and the left lifting eye of the turret are seen from the left rear of the turret. To the lower right are the turret ventilator hood and its splash guard. *John Charvat*

The black-colored cushion and the latching mechanism on the inner side of the loader's hatch door are seen close-up. In the background is the cupola, the front of which faces toward the right. Thus, the commander's machine gun is offset to the right side of the cupola. *John Charvat*

The cupola's hatch cover was designed either to swivel open to a position 90 degrees from horizontal, or to "pop up," remaining in a horizontal position a few inches above the top of the cupola. This was to allow the commander to have all-around outside vision while remaining protected from air-burst shells or fire from overhead. *John Charvat*

The IDF-type low-profile cupola had three M17 periscopes for the commander, the hinged covers of which are present on the top ledge of the cupola. The periscopes faced to the front and to both sides; a rear periscope was not included. A grab handle is welded to the hatch cover. *John Charvat*

The ring-shaped splash guard situated around the ventilator hood on the turret helped prevent splinters and small projectiles from penetrating the space below that hood, through which air was drawn into the ventilator. Fastened to the side of the stowage basket on the turret bustle is a holder for a fire extinguisher. *John Charvat*

The left armored top-loading air cleaner, including one of the elbow-shaped air intakes on the front of it, is in view, as well as details of the track connectors, track-support rollers, and, toward the lower right, the friction snubber (as the device that looks like a shock absorber is termed) for the rear bogie. *John Charvat*

The arrangement of the air cleaner (*left*) and the rear stowage box on the left fender of an M48A5 is depicted. To the right is the left rear lifting eye, which is welded to the armor of the hull. Fastened with hex nuts to the rear of the air cleaner is the air outlet, which conducts air from the air cleaner to the engine compartment. *John Charvat*

This overall view of an M48A5 from the left side emphasizes the low profile of the IDF-style cupola. This feature and the 105 mm gun barrel, with its center-mounted bore evacuator and lack of a muzzle brake, immediately distinguish this tank from 90 mm armed M48s. *John Charvat*

Most M48A5s were assigned to the National Guard and US Army Reserve, but approximately 140 of them served in the Republic of Korea in the late 1970s. M48A5 tanks in Korea serving with 1st and 2nd Battalions, 72nd Armor, had M2 .50-caliber machine guns for the tank commanders and M60D 7.62 mm MGs for the loaders. M239 smoke grenade launchers were attached to the turret face circa 1979. When 1-72 and 2-72 converted to M60A3s in the mid-1980s, the loader's pintle mounts and M60Ds were removed from the M48A5s and used on the M60A3s. Most later M48A5s used by various Army National Guard units had an M60D both for the tank commander and the loader. *John Charvat*

A rear view of an M48A5 exhibits common features of that model, including the socket for the side machine gun for the loader and the IDF-type cupola. The hinges of the cupola hatch cover are in view. Above the right fender is an exterior telephone box, also called a handset box.

The tow pintle of this M48A5 is rotated about 90 degrees from its normal vertical axis. To the sides of the tow pintle are the two square transmission-access plates, and above the pintle is the round transmission-access plate.

The left rear grille door of the M48A5 is shown in close detail. To the lower left of the grille door is the curved shield that helps deflect mud thrown to the inboard side and to the rear by the track; a similar shield is on the right side. Note the small screws and nuts that secure the shield to the hull.

The right-rear grille door is seen close-up, with a good view of the pentagonal fitting at the upper left for attaching a deepwater-wading trunk. Some of the upper louvers are crumpled. To the lower right is the right mud shield. *John Charvat*

In another rear view of an M48A5, the heavy-duty guard for the taillight assembly is in view. Also noticeable are the strips of steel that were welded to various parts of the frames of the grille doors for added strength.

The positioning of the external telephone box above the rear of the fender is demonstrated in this view. The rubber pads of the T142 tracks are severely worn, and the track assemblies of this M48A5 were camouflage-painted along with the rest of the tank when it received its restoration.

The external telephone box, or handset box, is seen from the side above the rear of the right fender. The right-rear lifting eye of the hull is between the telephone box and the right-rear storage box. Below the telephone box is the outboard end of the rear outrigger of the fender. The outriggers were numbered, and this one is number 6 (*right*). *John Charvat*

On each side of the turret below the rear lifting eye are two brackets for storing two tow cables. Each clamp held a cable adjacent to the eye, with the cables stretched around the rear of the turret. Each bracket is U shaped with an L-shaped pin through it; a retainer chain is connected to each pin and bracket. *John Charvat*

The right air cleaner of an M48A5 is viewed from the roof of the turret, which is traversed to the rear (to the right is the gun-shield dustcover). Both of the elbow-shaped air intake pipes at the front of the air cleaner are in view. *John Charvat*

The same air cleaner is seen from above the rear deck. Toward the right of the photo, between the air cleaner and the rear stowage box, is outrigger number 5, part of the structures for supporting the fender. This outrigger has three large lightening holes in it. *John Charvat*

An M48A5 is viewed from the right side. The M48A5s were powered by the Continental AVDS-1790-2D V-12 supercharged diesel engine through a General Motors CD-850-6A transmission with two forward ranges and one reverse. *John Charvat*

Above the fender of the M48A5 and to the front of the forward storage box is the exhaust pipe for the personnel heater. The positioning of the exhaust for the M60-type personnel heater to the right of the driver's hatch was a feature that was introduced with the M48A3. *John Charvat*